SOUTHERN WHITE GIRL SEEKS SOCIAL CHANGE

A TWENTIETH CENTURY MEMOIR

SOUTHERN WHITE GIRL SEEKS SOCIAL CHANGE

A TWENTIETH CENTURY MEMOIR

NANCY STOLLER

Southern White Girl Seeks Social Change: A Twentieth Century Memoir
© 2018, Nancy Stoller

ISBN 978-1-938007-12-5

Book Design by Stewart A. Williams.
Photographs, courtesy of Stoller family.

ACKNOWLEDGEMENTS

My thanks to everyone who made this book possible:

My San Francisco writing group: Molly Martin, Pam Pierce, and Chude Allen, who stuck with me for three years, while I wrote and re-wrote.

My Merrill Gardens Rockridge writing group: Suzanne Barba, Gloria Crocker, Alice Sachs, and Judy Pivar, who listened closely to everything I had to say.

Friends: You know who you are! But especially Helen, Sandy, Fish, Estelle, E.G., Cheri, Cookie, Lori, Bea, Amy, Liat, Susan, Dalit, Rochelle, Yvonne, Jon, Brian, Debbie, Sally, Barbara, Julie-Dodd, Marie-Laure, Annie, and Beth.

Family: Especially Gwendolyn, Bob, Peter, John, Isaiah, Lili, Ben, Sam, and Michael.

My physical therapists: Laura Pischetti and Morgan Crandall, thank you for believing in me.

A special thank you to Susie Bright, who took on the task of publishing this memoir without knowing the future.

TABLE OF CONTENTS

PART I
THE ROUTE TO ACTIVISM

1 New York Jews Dropped Into the Not-So-New South 3
2 The Twins and the Tomboy. 9
3 How I Became Jewish 17
4 Learning to Argue 37
5 What It's Like: Racism in Hampton 49

PART II
SOUTHERN YANKEE IN THE DIXIE COURT

6 Bowling for Freedom 64
7 It's in the BAG 74
8 The Tools are Imagination, Time, and Energy 80
9 Teaching at the Crossroads Baptist Church. 86
10 The Voter Registration Story: A Case of "Making it Up" 90
11 After Mort 104
12 How I Became a Certified Activist Intellectual 112
13 Arkansas Traveler 117

PART III
SOCIAL LOCATION PAINS

14 The One Who Is Born on Saturday 128
15 Motherhood and Personhood 136
16 The 24-Hour Day 141
17 Mexico and Morocco 152
18 Learning Balance and Stability 160
19 Troublemaker in the Academy. 164
20 Creating Child Care: "The Best Laid Plans of White Women..." 174
21 How to Unravel a Marriage 181
22 Moving On 193

PART I

THE ROUTE TO ACTIVISM

CHAPTER 1

NEW YORK JEWS DROPPED INTO
THE NOT-SO-NEW SOUTH

T he New York City newlyweds got off the train near the tip
of the Middle Peninsula of the Virginia delta. Riding in the
taxi to their one-bedroom, third-floor apartment in a converted house, they passed the Newport News Shipbuilding
and Drydock Company, and could see the battleships the company was creating. Mort pointed out Fort Monroe at the tip of
the peninsula. It had been a US Army base since the Civil War.
Ruth looked across the water toward Norfolk, where a naval
base was being expanded.

It was late October, 1939. Europe was at war, and two years
later, the United States would be also. Neither Mort nor Ruth
were Southerners or felt at home in the South, but they were
about to spend 21 years and raise three children here.

Mort had been living with a work colleague in Hampton
since August first. His new, and hopefully permanent, job was
as an electrical engineer for the National Advisory Committee
for Aeronautics. The agency had assigned him to its research

station at Langley Field, located at an Air Force base. His first assignment would be to improve rocket aerodynamics. The National Advisory Committee for Aeronautics that would become NASA gave him a half-day of vacation leave for each month he worked. As soon as he had accumulated a full day, he took a Friday morning train to New York. On a cool Saturday in November, he and Ruth were married, and on Sunday, they returned to their newly rented apartment in Hampton, about five miles from Langley.

✦

Both Mort and Ruth were products of New York City's progressive education system: free public schools, as well as free colleges. The only son of a gem setter who had immigrated to the US as a child from Chisinau, Moldova, Mort went to City College. At that time, even the texts were free in all the city-run colleges and graduate schools. Mort graduated with his electrical engineering degree in 1938, but had to search for a year to find an appropriate job. Until then, he drove a laundry truck.

Ruth, like Mort, was the first in her family to go to college. Her mother, Bessie, had been born in Bursztyn, Galicia, in 1888. Bessie was barely literate, but if she moved a pen slowly, she could sign her name in English. Ruth's father, Joseph, also from Burstyn, made a good living for his wife and three children by buying groceries wholesale and delivering them to little stores, at first by horse-drawn cart and later by truck. Joseph and Bessie met through a mutual assistance organization of Burstyn immigrants living on the Lower East Side. After Joseph's death in 1933, Ruth's young adult brothers took over the family business for a while. One got involved in managing apartments; the other eventually sold insurance. Ruth dropped out of Hunter College's pre-med program in 1938 after her junior year because, as she said many years later, "I knew Mort and I were going to get married as soon as he got a good job. I just didn't realize it would take a year. Besides, no one thought it was important to have a degree if you were a woman who was getting married."

Ruth had no idea how to cook, and of course, while Mort was at work, this was supposed to be one of her important responsibilities as a wife. Bessie had not allowed her in the kitchen to prepare meals. Ruth and Mort went out to dinner every night for the first week, walking from their small attic walkup in one of the grand old houses on Queens Street to a small restaurant a few blocks away. Finally, Ruth bought *The Settlement House Cookbook* and made her first dinner: meatloaf. According to our family narrative, the result was barely edible, but Mort ate it anyway.

This was the first day in Ruth's self-taught homeschooling to become a competent chef. She pursued this goal with the enthusiasm and élan of the chemistry major she had just been. Her strategy: "Use a cookbook like a lab manual!" *The Settlement House Cookbook* explained everything from how to boil water to the nutritional values of beans and meats to how to use an icebox. This advice manual was followed by the *Joy of Cooking*, which she used for guidance on everything culinary: how to set a table for eight guests, fourteen ways to prepare and complement a roast, six appropriate menus for an afternoon tea.

The couple apparently had a happy life exploring the locale from their treetop apartment. A photo from this period shows Mort flying a radio-controlled airplane and Ruth watching in one of her stylish, recently homemade dresses. (While no one had taught her how to cook, she did know how to sew.)

By a little more than a year after their marriage, Ruth was pregnant with twins. Ruth's mother was a twin, and the gene for twins apparently runs in our family, skipping a generation. My identical twin brothers were born March 4, 1941.

The third-floor walk-up was immediately overcrowded, and managing was difficult. Bringing two infants and a stroller down two steep flights of stairs in order to walk to the store was hard enough. Bringing the babies, the groceries, and the stroller back up was even more challenging.

The search began for a new place to live, preferably on ground level. In June, the family moved to Stuart Gardens, one of several Newport News housing developments built expressly for families of workers in the shipyard and other military industries. With two bedrooms, a small living room, a kitchen, and a bathroom, their shoebox house was exactly like 40 others in its neighborhood, and it was perfect for the family.

Only four months later, Ruth was pregnant again, this time with me, Nancy. It required another move. Our family found a house with three bedrooms on a large lot in Hampton. After purchasing the home for $6,000 in the fall of 1942, our family stayed there for 17 years until my father was transferred to Washington, DC to serve as part of the management team for the newly created NASA.

And so I grew up at 37 Alleghany Road.

Hampton is situated on a low-lying peninsula, shaped like my favorite childhood food: the salt stick. The peninsula is about ten miles long and perhaps five miles wide at the largest point. Our salt stick was connected to the rest of Virginia at its northwest end. At its southeast end, the peninsula jutted into Hampton Roads, a large inlet at the mouth of Chesapeake Bay. We lived in the Virginia Delta, hundreds of square miles of rich bottom land that went from the Atlantic to Richmond, where the land began to rise. Numerous rivers meandered through the delta and out to the ocean. Hampton, with a mean elevation of ten feet, was located between the York and James Rivers at the tip of its peninsula. All the nearby rivers ended in Chesapeake Bay, which linked them to the Atlantic. Inland from us on our peninsula were Yorktown, Williamsburg, and Jamestown, all famous early British settlements. Our own town, though primarily known in my youth for its crabbing industry and as the home of Hampton Institute (one of the early Freedman's Bureau colleges), also claimed its historical fame as the "oldest continuous English-speaking settlement in the New World." I had to repeat that phrase again and again in public school.

Tobacco and peanuts were still widely grown on plantations a few miles inland from Hampton. The racial atmosphere was Deep South. Schools and public accommodations of all types were segregated. Blacks rode in the back of the bus, and the word "nigger" was frequently used in white society, although it was forbidden in my family. The Civil War battle between the Merrimac and the Monitor, two early iron-clad steam-driven battleships, had been fought about a half-mile from shore in a direct sight line from our house: my home from three months old until I graduated from high school in 1959.

My parents were a particular brand of Jew: liberal, anti-segregationist, and rationalist. Both were also scientists, atheists, and Yankees. Consequently, they were never fully part of the local white culture and were marginal to the southern Jewish world as well. On the other hand, they were married, lived a middle-class lifestyle, had three (cute) well-behaved children, and didn't drink or do drugs.

Plus, my mother was active in the PTA, the League of Women Voters, and the Girl Scouts. So in some ways, we did fit in.

Ruth did manage to cause trouble, however, through her participation in several liberal civic organizations. As president of our elementary school PTA, she opposed youth football, a move that caused humiliation and harassment for my brothers and I. Then, together with several friends, she helped desegregate both the League of Women Voters and the local Girl Scout Council. As her children, we were proud of her, in a sort of nascent pre-political, stand-up-for-your-parents way, but her actions help to explain why no one would believe I wasn't *really* a Yankee, even when I explained that I had been born in Newport News Hospital and raised "right here."

CHAPTER 2

THE TWINS AND THE TOMBOY

From the time I could walk, and perhaps even before then, all I wanted was to do was hang out with my brothers. In fact, I wanted to be one of them; I fought as hard as I could to be the third twin.

If these two can do it, I thought, why not me?

Their twin-hood meant that they were special just by being. Identical and very cute with their curly bright red hair, green eyes, and freckles, everyone admired them wherever we went. Until third grade, my mother dressed them the same: there were some color variations, but they always wore the same patterns and styles, the same blue pants and button-up jackets.

My main memory of being on the street with them and my mother is the experience of having another woman smile broadly and say, "Oh, the twins!" Then a pause. "...and Nancy." In the social world of the 1940s, twins were much more interesting than a blonde singleton. Acknowledging me was a matter of politeness, but it seemed there was nothing special in my appearance.

For my brothers, the biggest challenge may have been to

be recognized as individuals. For me, the struggle was to be noticed at all. One role I adopted was the final arbiter of who was Bob and who was Pete, both in life and in photos. Even as an adult, I've found myself maintaining this position. For years, I held that I was better at Stoller twin identification than they were, because I had years of direct comparative viewing experience that they lacked. I still always want to feel necessary to their twin lives.

Within our household, however, we were all treated equally. I knew my options to be "more important" were limited there. Outside of our home, I tried to be the most athletic, the best tree climber, and the fastest runner among us. Once we were in school, I worked hard to be the best student.

Perhaps because they were identical twins, Bob and Pete were naturally ambidextrous. In school, however, they were forced to right-handedness. They had started first grade at five years old, not uncommon in those days, but were both forced to repeat that year because they couldn't get their writing to a sufficient quality for promotion. At this point, I was promoted from kindergarten to first grade in the same school. So we progressed through elementary and secondary school all in the same grade, reinforcing our closeness, but possibly damaging our relationship somewhat at the same time; I was proud to be ahead of my age group, and they had to explain why their younger sister was in the same grade—and sometimes getting *better* grades.

In my ongoing attempts to be recognized, I would bring my report cards home and boast about my good grades, hoping I would be praised above my brothers. Inevitably I was told that I should work harder (or a similar platitude), and that we each did the best we could. I felt I would never be special at home. So I rededicated myself at school, seeking and finding as many high grades and teacher approvals as I could.

I have no memories of playing with dolls. I did have stuffed animals, including a dachshund I got in junior high, that I used to collect autographs of friends. The only girly things I remember liking were coloring books and fingerpaints.

All the girls I knew played in their houses, or close by. They had little interest in the activities I liked: softball, touch football, climbing trees, beach combing. I was willing to play in the yard...mine, theirs, anywhere. The further I could get from the inside of my own home, the better. To me, the household interior was a place of chores or reading and games with my brothers. If they weren't there and free to play with me, being inside was boring. My preferred companions were my brothers, their friends, or the girl up the street, who was a tomboy.

Tomboys seemed very rare in Hampton. Being a tomboy was easy. Most of the children and young teenagers on our street were boys. All I had to do was follow my brothers to find my natural environment.

We all three idolized our across-the-street neighbor, B.B. Hudgins, who was about ten years our senior. We were similarly fascinated by the Braxton brothers, Elliot and Phil, who lived on the corner next to B.B. By the time we were in elementary school, Elliot was off at college; Phil followed a few years later. We eagerly visited whenever they were in town. From B.B. and Phil, I got my four childhood nicknames: Twin, Sister, Isabelle, and Stonewall. Twin was obvious. Sister was a common nickname for girls in the South, especially within the extended family. Since our neighbors had no sisters, giving me this name was partly a sort of fictional family connection and partly a way of calling me by my family role, just as "Twin" was the family role, or identity, of my brothers. The origin of Isabelle was—and still is—a mystery to me. Stonewall, however, referred to Thomas Edward Jackson, a Confederate general, who got his nickname for his toughness during the Civil War. As a child, I loved this nickname because I liked to think of myself as tough and tenacious. I only knew it was for "a general as tough as a stone wall."

"Hey, Twin!" and "Hey, Stonewall!" were the two sweetest sounds to my ears.

But when I found out in high school that Jackson was a Confederate, I suffered classic liberal white Southern inner conflict. I liked the nickname, but not the association. So I buried the nickname away. When asked later if I had any nicknames as a child, I would only mention this one if I had time for a long explanation and a request not to use it. In 2015, while hiking the Camino Santiago and looking for an old nickname to use in our group, I picked Sister, even though the first name to come to mind was, of course, Stonewall.

B.B. taught us to enjoy the beach and Hampton Roads. He showed us kayaking, rowing, how to use an outboard motor, and the right technique for hunting at the duck blinds. Elliott taught us magic tricks upstairs in a huge attic filled with old furniture and leather-covered chests; Phil introduced us to the Ouija board. The Braxtons seemed a little strange in an old-fashioned Southern way, which wasn't surprising, since they were descended from signers of the Declaration of Independence. Their household was mysterious, what I would now call "Victorian gothic" (magic tricks, Ouija board). Their father was friendly, but their mother was hostile; she also had a close friend who lived in their huge house with them.

While in his mid-twenties, Elliott died mysteriously in Greece. Once I was old enough to know what "gay" was, I decided that he had been gay and that his long stay in Greece, followed by the death that no one wanted to discuss, was connected. In his twenties, Phil became entwined with an evangelical cult whose weekly services had been frequented by his mother and her friend for many years, and disappeared into the religion. B.B., on the other hand, graduated from University of Virginia as a young alcoholic who was never able to keep a job. Eventually his parents forced him to leave home. Our older friends on Alleghany Road had basically moved on in ways we knew that we wouldn't.

My brothers were not typical "southern boys." Although we played touch football and simple softball in our backyard with other kids our age, my mother opposed competitive sports, especially violent ones. No Little League or Pop Warner football for my brothers. And to save money, we were not encouraged to take any afterschool lessons, beyond learning the basics of how to swim one summer in Charlottesville, where my father was studying for his master's degree in Electrical Engineering. I missed most of the swimming lessons due to severe ear infections. For the rest of my life, I've hesitated to put my head underwater in a pool, convinced that the water carries some kind of bacteria that are attracted to my eardrums.

Our outdoor activities in Hampton focused more on boating and scouting. I would have preferred to be a Boy Scout, like my brothers, but that wasn't an option, so into Brownies and then Girl Scouts I went, doing every outdoor activity I could.

I didn't want to be a boy—the anatomy looked too dangerous to me. I had always been warned not kick my brothers "down there." They could be permanently damaged. And certainly their penises didn't look very protected. I knew I didn't want one. I did want everything a boy had socially: the right to run around without supervision; to play team sports; to wear pants to school and parties; and to have short hair. I wanted to be an androgynous boy. All of my boyfriends—and most of my girlfriends after I became a lesbian—fit an androgynous format: flat-chested, not too much body hair, medium to light-weight. Sometimes I think that women appealed to me because they were not-men. As a child, I thought of men as big, hairy, bulky, and a bit scary. Being a happy tomboy began my own perhaps narcissistic attraction to other tomboys.

In elementary and secondary school, I was required to wear skirts or dresses, always against my will. I considered any clothing with a skirt to be ridiculous, designed to keep girls from doing all sorts of interesting things: climbing trees, fences, sheds, walls, boulders; riding a bike freely; playing sports; running; doing cartwheels; even leaning over. Fortunately, my parents had no objection to my wearing pants every day after school and on the weekends. Plus, my dressing like a boy helped the household budget. I could wear my brothers' hand-me-downs when I went out to play. Of course, this made me even happier by reinforcing my twin connection.

Later, after graduating from high school, I still wore blue jeans and a t-shirt or a black turtleneck whenever possible, pulling on a skirt only when it was required for tea or Sunday dinner at my college. To this day, my favorite clothes are sneakers, white socks, blue jeans, a short sleeve tee, and a flannel shirt. As I sit here typing, that's what I'm wearing. Now, at 73, I wear my hair in a crew cut with a small flip at the front, just as I always wished I could back then, when I usually had braids or a ponytail.

There were only two girls near my age in our immediate neighborhood. Patsy Womble lived up the street, just past the marsh creek. She was two years younger than me and easily manipulated. I convinced her to try "squeeze-together sex" in her bedroom when we were eight and six. She didn't have many ideas of her own to contribute for outdoor – or indoor – play.

The other girl, Lynne Lively, lived in a white multi-porch house diagonally behind ours. I could walk through a scratchy opening in the hedge into her backyard. Lynne's father sold real estate; her mother stayed home and beautified the house. Lynne was always a total femme; she played dress-up and dolls, took dance lessons, didn't want to get dirty, and was forbidden to leave her yard. Boring, boring, boring. Occasionally, on desperate rainy days, I would join her to share crayons and fill in the images in our coloring books. Then we might play Monopoly or Parcheesi, or try to make checkers interesting.

I knew the religion of every friend's family; Lynne's was Presbyterian. I think her parents might not have liked that my family was Jewish. This may be one reason that she never came to play at our house. They put up with me, I think, because all of Lynne's other friends lived too far away to just walk over.

JoAnn Wood, who lived a bike ride away, had a stay-at-home mother who made pottery. Her father was an archaeologist at Williamsburg, twenty miles away. I was repeatedly shocked by his meanness and his physical abuse of his children. Based on my own family experience, which I'd been told was normal, I thought that scientists simply did not use brute force on their children. And I had absorbed my parents' class-biased view, that only the poor and ignorant beat their children. JoAnn would sometimes miss school because her bruises were too severe for her to walk, and when she finally came back, we could still see the stripes across the backs of her legs. Her three younger siblings suffered the same treatment. In junior high, she was forever being punished with full restriction for a week for some minor offense. She couldn't go out, talk on the phone, or watch TV. For that week, she could do nothing except her homework, be silent, and stay in her room. She wasn't even supposed to read a book. This went on all the way through her teen years.

In the eighth grade, I met another tomboy, Gene Mercer. Her father was an army sergeant and a medic at Fort Monroe. A horrible bully, he pulled out Gene's front baby teeth when he thought it was time for them to go. Gene told me that a friend of his was present when her father did this to her. He also beat up Gene's mom several times a week. His wife was so submissive, even to me, that I couldn't understand why anyone would hit her. Sergeant Mercer had named his daughter Gene because he wanted a boy. His second child, a boy, was allowed to do as he wished, and after the parents were finally divorced, the son took over his father's role as bully to his mother.

From JoAnn's and Gene's families, I learned what terrible things could go on behind middle-class doors. With Gene, I would wander the streets as much as possible so she wouldn't have to go home. JoAnn, on the other hand, could hardly leave her house.

❖

My closest female friend in high school was Mary Beth Olsen. We shared most secrets, rode the bus home from school together, and spent the night together whenever possible. Mary Beth also had a super secret wild life that she didn't share with me for several years. She had two lovers, both students at our high school; one was Jewish and intellectual, while the other was a football star. Every so often, I would cover for her when she went out with the Jewish boyfriend because her parents were blatantly anti-Semitic. It never occurred to me that she was having sex with both guys! Only after both relationships were over, when we were both in college, did she reveal the truth.

My own sex life was ultra quiet. There had been a dorky, pre-pubescent boyfriend in junior high, who I'd kissed twice to see what it was like. Then I had a great friendship with Carl Hacker, another science student and teenage intellectual. In high school, we shared a few kisses and many talks. In a book for our 25th reunion, I found out that he and I were the only two people in our class to get doctorates. I wondered if we had encouraged each other in that ambition. Although I thought having sex with someone might be fun, I was terrified of getting pregnant, so I put that off for some future time: "probably in my mid-twenties," I thought.

CHAPTER 3

HOW I BECAME JEWISH

I was born a Jew, but it wasn't until I was six that I began the tedious and frustrating process of becoming Jewish.

Bob, Pete, and I were playing in the street. As usual when not in school, all three of us were in blue jeans and t-shirts. I was five and my brothers were six. It was hot, hot, hot: a mid-summer Sunday. In Hampton, people bragged that "the humidity matches the temperature." By the start of July, the temperature was usually over 80 degrees by 11 in the morning, and here it was 1:30 in the afternoon.

We were on the far side of the road from our house, pulling up the grit-filled tar, each of us trying to tease the gravel out before biting down to pop the bubbles. Ouch! A little piece of sand felt like it was breaking the top of my back tooth.

I looked up to see Ray Womble pedaling casually toward us from up the street, where his house was nestled on our favorite creek and marsh. To get our attention, he screeched his bicycle to a sudden halt, just barely staying vertical. He still had on his white shirt from church, but his good pants had been replaced with jeans. He was only one day from his Saturday crew cut, probably a Number 1 in the electric razor setting. Even though I was only five, I already envied his buzz cut. I was wearing braids, which my mother had recently taught me to do myself, thus depriving me of the one activity in which she touched me in a nurturing fashion. (Otherwise, there were only practical connections: "Here's your coat." "Let me measure the hem on that dress.")

"What are you all doing?" Ray wanted to know.

"Just playing."

"In your old clothes? Didn't you go to church?"

"We don't go to church," said Pete. "We're Jewish." (We had all been taught how to answer that question, a useful thing to know since we were the only Jewish kids for at least a mile, maybe more, in any direction.)

"You're Jewish?" Ray's eyes seemed to get brighter. "Jews, I know about them. They killed Christ."

I didn't know who Christ was exactly. I knew he had something to do with church, and that he was a person who everyone in Hampton seemed to think had been *really* important back in history. His full name was "Jesus Christ" and no one, even us non-Christians, was allowed to say his name in surprise or anger, as in, "Jesus Christ, that hurt!" I didn't think that anyone in my family had killed him. Wouldn't our parents have told us if something like that were true?

Timothy Sniffen, our backyard neighbor, was crossing the street to check on the tar bubble popping.

"Hey, Timothy, they killed Christ," said Ray.

Timothy seemed nonplussed, as if Ray hadn't spoken at all.

"They're Jews. They killed Christ!" Ray's voice got louder. Turning from Timothy, he focused his eyes on each of us in turn. "You killed Christ!" he chanted. "You killed Christ, you killed Christ, you killed Christ!"

Somehow, there seemed to be some weight behind his

words. It was as if he were taunting me with another version of, "You peed your pants!" It was one of those humiliating accusations that made me certain I had done the thing I was being accused of. Was it true? Did our grandparents, or someone before them, kill Jesus? Why did I feel like I was responsible for the death of Ray's Sunday morning icon, who was, even after centuries, still the peace-loving shepherd of everyone else in my town?

Meanwhile, Ray was continuing: "I'm gonna tell: you killed Christ!" It seemed like he wanted to fight, even though in our loose neighborhood world, he was a friend. Living only halfway up the block, he was always ready to join us to search the marsh for water snails and crabs, to play catch, climb a tree, visit, or have us play at his house. Getting together was just a matter of parental permission, which was easily obtained, as long as no one was under some temporary restriction.

We did have our unanticipated conflicts and petty fights, and this attack was like a lightning flash before thunder. The air got hotter still, especially around my forehead. My hair was in my eyes. I could feel sweat at the corners of my eyelids, and I had to squint at him through the bright sun.

"Did not!" I protested.

"Did too!"

"Did not!" My brothers joined in.

"Did too!"

"Did not!"

We were at our end of the block, and we outnumbered Ray three to one, but we were getting nowhere. Was he right?

Our relaxed feeling was gone. The tar was getting too hard to chew. Who could chew tar anyway under such conditions? And if it continued, who on the block would side with us? Did other kids or their parents (a more frightening group) think the same way as Ray? Or maybe the other kids hadn't yet discovered our shameful connection to Jesus? And now would Ray tell them?

"We're leaving," said Bob. I always followed my brothers' footsteps and directions. I turned immediately toward our house.

"*Nyah, nyah, nyah!* You killed Christ!" Ray yelled, as we walked as slowly and with as much dignity as we were able to muster back to our front porch. Our green screen door was calling us. Timothy walked with us. At the door, he said good-bye and walked around the side of our house to the opening in the low hedge, which led to the cottage in the next lot where his family lived.

Several years later, I realized that Timothy's family was the only family I knew in Hampton that was neither Jewish nor churchgoing. This meant that he was always one of us "outsiders." I think his father worked in a museum. Mr. Sniffen was a white-collar, scientist-intellectual, and therefore probably also suspect, just like my own parents. I was already embarrassed by Timothy's last name: Sniffen, so much like sniffling, something we never wanted to do in public. Even his first name, Timothy, seemed so formal and almost feminine. No one ever called him Tim. It was always Timothy.

Stepping inside our shade-filled front hall was like touching the tree in a game of tag. No one, especially not a six-year old, would dare mess with us while we were inside, nor would they enter without our permission and our mother's welcome. No matter what our grandparents had done.

We were safe, but what had happened, and what did it mean? Speaking over each other, we reported to our parents. Both were home because it was Sunday. They assured us that we didn't kill "Christ." In fact, the word "Christ" was just a name that people who now called themselves Christians gave to a man whose name was Jesus. Christians thought this Jesus was the (or "a") son of God. And he was killed by the Romans, not by Jews. The explanation was confusing. After all, did gods, or "God," have children that could be killed by regular people? And the experience in the street had also been scary. Ray had chanted, "*You* killed Christ," as if my brothers and I were directly responsible. That was definitely frightening.

Amid reassurances from our parents that the taunting was just ignorance on Ray's part, we played at home for the rest of the day, then were given dinner and put through our bedtime routines. Monday would be another day. This was not serious, we were told: just prejudice and ignorance.

My parents blamed most opinions they disagreed with on ignorance. It could be institutional racism, prejudice, stereotypes, bad attitudes about poor people, or even the belief that you had to eat kosher food. It was all due to ignorance. Rationality was the way to go. Both maintained this perspective throughout their lives.

What we children didn't anticipate that summer afternoon was that Mort and Ruth would continue to talk about what had happened, and about the best way to respond to it, over the next month.

Mort was convinced that they should just ignore it, or maybe talk to Ray's family. Of course, that task would have fallen to Ruth, since my father never actually engaged with any neighbors beyond those across the street or across the hedge. All his friends came from his own work colleagues. Ruth, however, thought that they should send us to the religious school of the local synagogue in downtown Hampton. Eventually she convinced Mort that this was the way to go. They joined the B'nai Israel congregation by paying a sum that would allow us to attend the school every week. My brothers and I were excluded from the decision.

After these discussions, my mother announced that in the fall we would start attending "Sunday school." At first, I thought this meant some Christian activity, since I knew that Jews did not go to church on Sunday. Only Christians went to Sunday school. Our parents explained that this Sunday school was a class for Jewish children, held at the synagogue at the same time that the Christians were in church. Why at that time, I wanted to know? I worried that going to Sunday school might turn me into a Christian, just as I thought that going into a church was dangerous. Didn't Christians "own" Sunday?

"Because Saturday morning, Jewish adults go to *shul*, so no one can teach you then. And during the week in the afternoon, there are the Hebrew classes...and we don't think you need them, at least not now."

Sunday school? Hebrew classes? Go to additional school instead of playing? What had we brought on ourselves by reporting the teasing? Maybe we should have just kept quiet.

There was no changing their minds. They had concluded their process, and they announced in a united front. We would go to Sunday school, so that we would "know about your history and be able to answer questions when people ask if you're Jewish or what the Jews did."

Writing this 65 years later, I realize that this conversation took place in 1947, only two years after the Holocaust ended. Between 1933 and 1945, all the known (and probably also the unknown) members of our family in Europe had been killed, simply because they were Jewish. Although they never discussed it, I'm sure my parents knew something about this. They did say later, when I would ask if they or other relatives ever went back to visit the places they came from, that those places no longer existed. I thought that meant that perhaps everyone had left these places in the early 1900s, or that the towns or cities had been bombed during WWII. I couldn't imagine that millions of people just like me had been killed during my own lifetime, and that if I had been born "there" I would probably be already dead. And my parents and brothers would be dead, too.

So without this knowledge, we began seven years of Sunday mornings in which one teacher after another tried to convince us of the truth of the Old Testament, the value of saying prayers in *shul*, and the importance of celebrating holidays at home. I responded with as much head-butting as possible against Judaism, religion in general, God, and my own nuclear family: the latter for their hypocritical behavior in sending us to this school which drilled us in ideas that they themselves rejected. It was even worse when I went through a period in early adolescence of wanting to celebrate the Jewish holidays to gain a sense of community belonging. My parents and brothers viewed me with disdain. Even I asked myself: "What *are* you doing?"

Every Sunday during the school year, one parent drove us to Sunday school, where we joined our cohort of similarly aged children for an hour and a half to "learn about Jewish history and the Jewish religion." The teachers and the rabbi seemed to assume that we, like the other children (I was sure we were the only "different ones") were eating kosher chicken on Friday evenings, consuming at least a box of matza every spring, and taking home tin menorahs for Chanukah every December. In our home however, the only identifiable Jewish things were scattered Yiddish phrases, borscht, stuffed cabbage, bagels and lox, and yearly summer trips to our New York City relatives.

Throughout my early childhood, the Holocaust was never directly discussed in Sunday school or in my nuclear or extended family in my presence as far as I can remember. Perhaps our parents wanted to shield us, though they must have been thankful that we were in the United States and not in Europe.

B'nai Israel synagogue was a small, white frame building on King Street, a few miles away in downtown Hampton. It had a sanctuary, a cloakroom, a toilet, an upper balcony for women, and a basement with a large room for parties and holiday meals.

There were small classrooms upstairs. I remember learning to play *dreidel* games in one of them and arguing about the book of Genesis in another.

Less than 100 people, comprising perhaps 35 families, belonged to the synagogue. The congregation was scattered around Elizabeth City County, of which Hampton was the county seat. The only synagogue in the county when I was young, B'nai Israel was Orthodox in orientation, but everyone – that is, all Jews, including our family's unacknowledged atheists – were welcome. The rabbi couldn't afford to set standards that the congregation couldn't meet.

I grew up believing that Jews were more liberal than most of the Christians in my town, although this belief was probably exaggerated somewhat by my own parents' differences from our neighbors. I think that perhaps ten of the synagogue's families were like mine. In one, the father was a Jew from a bigger northern city who had come south to work at N.A.C.A. When my father's Jewish work colleagues came to dinner, they talked about developing rockets, computer technology, and advanced airplanes and jets. (I don't remember any non-Jews at a parental dinner, ever.) They wore clip-on name tags to work and had radiation monitors on their belts. They built their own model airplanes, fantasized about supersonic flight, and discussed the chemical composition of stars.

I had the impression that these men were rationalists who had no real use for religion. I thought that perhaps their wives had also made them join the *shul*. In any event, even though I knew they were connected to the congregation somehow – through their children – I never saw them attend any service. My parents never went, either.

Most of the adult members of B'nai Israel were lawyers, doctors, store owners, and artisans. Maybe the person who ran the deli was also Jewish. I never asked, but I doubted a non-Jew would think to provide the NY Times every Sunday and sell bagels, lox, cream cheese, white fish, salt sticks, and halvah for displaced New Yorkers. Not likely.

My other childhood education in Judaism came on our yearly trips to New York. Both of my parents were from greater New York City, and since no other members of either extended family had moved further away than Long Island or New Jersey, every summer we piled into our Plymouth and journeyed north. We split our visits fairly evenly between my father's small family (his parents and two aunts) and my mother's larger group, which included my grandmother, two uncles, and eight cousins.

Sam and Anna Stoller lived in a tidy section of Queens. Their single-family home had space for an incredibly neat garden and fishpond. Dinners were at an elaborately set round table with linen, beautiful plates, stemware, and real silver service. In the basement, where my brothers and I slept on skinny cots and a sagging horsehair sofa, my grandfather had his tiny gem-setting workshop. When we were lucky, he'd allow us to stand quietly behind him as he picked up rubies and emeralds with a dark beeswax cone and set them in ring findings or earrings, transforming a gold or silver skeleton into a glowing flower. He showed us the soft leather pouch in which he carried stones worth thousands of dollars back and forth to his downtown employer. Both grandparents, especially my grandmother, were strange to me. She seemed afraid we would break something at any minute: a message frequently reinforced by my mother, and one that made me almost unable to eat because I was sure that my hand and a tall, thin glass would collide at any moment. Seeing my father tap a knife to a glass to let us hear the sound of crystal only further stiffened me at the table. On one visit, someone *did* knock a glass over, but it did not break. We children scrambled to the living room and then waited in the yard while the adults mopped up the water.

The tension generated by three young children in the house intensified my usual desire to be outside. My favorite outdoor activity was lying on my stomach, chin over the edge of the pond, watching the goldfish. This, of course, made my grandmother fear that I was about to fall in – or that even if I didn't end up in the pond, I would at least ruin my clothes.

When visiting these grandparents, we usually left early every morning to stop by the museums of my parents' youth. This part was heaven. We went to the Museum of Natural History, our favorite, at least once each year. I learned every hall to the point that I could tell whether a new exhibit was up or an old one gone from the previous year.

Our parents also dragged us to at least two art museums each year. These were my mother's favorites. She felt it was important that we walk through the Metropolitan Museum of Art, where we always visited the mummies and spent time with the knights. I went as quickly as possible through the religiously themed work; I knew that this Christian stuff wasn't for me, and it was also excessively repetitious and boring. We spent more time in the modern art galleries, which my mother tried to explain. My own favorites were the early 20th-century Russians: Chagall, Tchelichew, and Kandinsky.

At the Museum of Modern Art, I realized that the prints on the hall stairs in our own house were copies of real paintings by Picasso, Leger, Gaugin, and Miró. Perhaps my mother had bought her prints during a visit to this museum when I was younger and then posted them at 37 Alleghany Road to remind her of the city. When I was sixteen, a senior in high school, a student took some photos for the yearbook on those Alleghany Road stairs. I was acutely embarrassed that one of the prints was Picasso's *Nude before a Mirror*. The woman's breasts and belly were so obvious that I felt our advisor was certain to crop the photo for obscene content. (He either didn't notice or didn't care, because when the final version of the 1959 Newport News High School yearbook came out, there they were.)

We also traveled to the architectural icons of New York: the Statue of Liberty, the Empire State Building, Rockefeller Center. We ate weird food and went to weird restaurants; I always insisted on at least one giant pretzel from the street vendor in front of the Natural History Museum, but was revolted at the thought that New Yorkers ate them with mustard. Where did they get these strange ideas? When my father ushered us into the Horn and Hardart Automated Cafeteria, I thought I'd entered a futuristic science fiction restaurant. A quarter or two in a slot unlocked a glass door to a sandwich or a glass of chocolate milk! I wanted to eat every meal at Horn and Hardart.

Clearly, New Yorkers lived in a far more interesting world than did Hamptonians. I was beginning to think that New York was my real home, not Hampton, Virginia. This, I thought, is how Jews live when they can. They go to museums, read books, attend plays, enjoy neon, and love science. In New York, we were normal, while in Hampton, our interests, values, and religion marked us as strange outsiders.

However, if our first week's day trips to Manhattan were glorious, the second week of the yearly vacation was twisted, painful, and confusing. While the Stollers lived a kind of cautious life with aristocratic values, the Klarbergs of Bayside, Long Island, seemed to be obsessed with whether our branch of the family was Jewish enough. Adding to their relentless criticism of the Hampton branch of the family, Uncle Manny and Aunt Betty's home – where we always stayed for one long week – was filled with internal conflicts.

Ruth had two older brothers, Nat and Manny. According to her, they fought incessantly when she was young, both with each other and with their father. The fights were physical. She told me about trying to separate them many times. She also believed that their fighting had somehow helped to kill her father, who had died when she was only sixteen. The diagnosis had been colon cancer.

During my youth, the words "cancer" and "colon" were both forbidden in polite company. As a child, I believed that a "stomach problem" had killed my grandfather. As an adult, I got a little more information and wrote "stomach cancer" repeatedly on medical history forms, until I discovered the precise diagnosis from my mother when I was already in my fifties. In my mother's version of events, Joseph's sons' verbal and physical attacks weakened him during his long illness and demise. In her own childrearing, she forbade any back talk, because she connected it with the violence of her brothers toward her father.

In the 1940s and 1950s, when we were visiting them every summer, Nat and Manny fought very little with each other. They worked in separate spheres entirely. Nat was an accountant, while Manny ran a real estate practice, buying and renting buildings and houses. They lived about ten miles apart on opposite sides of Long Island. I rarely saw them together.

Nat was quieter; he and his wife Doris lived in Flushing in one of the most boring stretches of housing that I had ever seen. There were a few trees on a double lane road with too much traffic in front of their semi-detached house, no park nearby, and no yard at all beyond a small patio. Their idea of fun seemed to be watching television and playing cards. I discovered in Flushing that my mother and Bessie also both loved to play cards. In fact, it was Bessie who taught me how to play poker, to the shock of my Hampton friends; to many of them, *any* card playing was sinful, and poker, as a gambling game, was the worst kind. Nat and Doris' daughter, Jean Bonnie, was a year older than me and as boring as her parents. When she was young, her primary interests were clothes and dolls.

If Nat's house was boring, Manny's was chaotic and dangerous, and it was here that my parents housed us because there was "lots of space." Years later my mother told me that she would have preferred the peace of Flushing, but we had needed the space for the five of us.

Why was it so bad in Bayside? Put simply, Manny was a tall, heavily built bully who seemed to think it was funny to humiliate and dominate his diminutive wife Betty and their seven children. There were multiple alliances and conflicts among the children. Joan, the oldest, was protective of Nancy and Ellen, a middle and a young daughter; Carol, next in line, seemed to protect Steve, the next youngest after her. Susie, just a year younger than Steve, got some support also from Joan, but was always in trouble with Manny. Once when she was sixteen, Manny hit her so hard he broke her jaw. Michael, the youngest, was born too late to be swirled up in these alliances. Years later, Manny told Ellen that he used violence because that was how he had been brought up himself and that his own father had been brutal towards him and his brother.

Three of the children died before reaching forty. Nancy had been born prematurely. Always physically uncomfortable, she suffered throughout her life from severe skin rashes and a sun allergy. She died from stomach cancer in her early twenties. Following 1960s medical advice, her parents kept her own cancer diagnosis a secret from her, believing it was better for her not to know that she was dying.

At age nineteen, Susan, while living in Maryland (where she'd gone to college to escape her family), slit her wrists and swallowed pills, believing that because she was too masculine and that because she loved a woman, there was really no place for her in the world. Three days later she awoke, called 911, and wanted to live. Her parents had her institutionalized, first in a private hospital and then at Creedmoor State on Long Island.

They, and perhaps her therapists, thought she might be schizophrenic (the diagnosis reported to her family) in addition to being a lesbian. My cousins also thought for years that her lesbian desires might be a symptom of mental illness. Did she have shock treatment or take anti-psychotics? No one remembers. On June 9, 1969, nineteen days before the Stonewall Riots, she asphyxiated herself in her mother's car in the family's garage. She was twenty years old.

Michael, who was diagnosed as bipolar, became an ultra-orthodox Jew in his thirties. He died one night at his apartment, which was owned by his religious community. For years, I thought that the cause of his death had been an incorrect ingestion of pills. I learned last year that it was in fact probably due to his quitting his lithium and then stopping his thyroid medication, perhaps because he was depressed. His body probably slowed down to a halt, and he evidently died from starvation. He was found three days after his death in his apartment, lying in bed. Was it suicide? Unclear.

In the Bayside of my youth, these three cousins were all still alive, though moving toward their early deaths. While staying there, we would visit my grandmother Bessie at her house a few miles away, go to the beach, or visit a nearby swimming pool. I was introduced to Coney Island, Far Rockaway, and the Atlantic Ocean of the northern states. And I was able to try to play the piano: a big thrill, since my mother was convinced that none of her children could carry a tune and music lessons for us were worthless.

At the Klarberg household at 220th St. in Bayside, we were also continually immersed in daily family dramas and crises. Almost every day, I saw fighting, manipulation, and dissembling. I watched my cousins pointedly ignoring others who spoke to them. They could be harsh on us visitors too. I was teased about my southern accent. I was quizzed about living in the midst of so many Gentiles. How could I stand it? (It seemed normal to me. My cousins, though, *did* seem strange.) The Bayside house was frightening to me; I felt claustrophobic. There was nowhere to relax on foot outside, either, just square blocks of brick two-story houses, empty sidewalks, dogs on leashes, and streets full of cars going somewhere unknown.

The food and the style of eating were also different from home. I remember thirteen or fourteen of us (the eight or nine Klarbergs, always with a baby in a high chair, and five Stollers) crowded in a small dining room with big bowls of potatoes, green vegetables, a giant roast or a turkey, and my cousin Carol eating chunks of meat and pulling the last shreds off the bone. Joan acted as a second mother, serving and keeping things moving. Betty sat at one end of the table, pregnant but always in charge in that supervisory way of the boss who has left directions and expects them to be followed. The girls seemed to do all the work, and Steve did just as he wished.

The family acted out their ongoing conflicts at the table. Several times, Susie left in tears after some exchange with her father. No one seemed willing to ally with her, at least not in front of us. When discussing plans for Steve's *bar mitzvah*, Manny turned on my brothers. Why weren't they getting *bar mitzvahed*? And why weren't they going to Hebrew school? Didn't they have Hebrew school down there? My father would explain, again, that he had left the decision about *bar mitzvahs* – and Hebrew school – up to my brothers, and they didn't want to do either. This resulted in more criticism of my parents, something that I had never seen or heard before. I silently sided with them completely. I knew that the only reason my dad had been *bar mitzvahed* back in New York in 1930 was that his own grandfather had wanted it. Neither his father nor he supported the rituals of Judaism. The Stollers were New World, rational, scientific, and atheistic Jews; they were not going to perpetuate this Old World custom.

I wondered if the Bayside part of my family represented what most Jews were like. My uncle certainly fit one stereotype of the pushy, loud, conflict-loving, and materialistic Jew. In Bayside, I also saw an exaggeration of the sexism I was learning in Sunday school; that men have more privileges than women. To them, women should stand back, take care of the household, and let men make all the mega-decisions, even about the children. Boys could aspire only to replicating their father's life – a career in real estate like Manny's, for example – while girls could become teachers or wives. This was so boring, depressing, and anti-democratic. I knew that this kind of Judaism, with its sexism, hostility, patriarchy, and acceptance of conflict and bullying, was not for me. If I were going to be Jewish, it would be different. I would be the Manhattan-oriented Jew of museums and science, and my Old World religious cultural identity would be avoided as much as possible.

When one turned twelve, Sunday school usually morphed into Hebrew lessons for boys, and even for some of the girls – although *bat mitzvahs* were not yet common in Virginia. All three of us stopped attending Sunday school. And that was the end of my involvement in anything institutionally Jewish for the next thirty years.

I'm thirteen. It's breakfast on a Saturday. Ruth and I are talking about the difference between being Jewish in an ethnic sense and being religious. She and Mort had often said that they were not religious. They didn't belong to the Jewish religion, but they were ethnically Jewish. Of course, they didn't belong to any other religion, and neither did I.

"Well," I asked, "are you an atheist?"

She stopped for a moment and then said, "No, I'm agnostic."

"What's that mean?" I asked.

"That means that I'm not sure; there might be a God and

there might not. I focus on other things in life."

I thought this was a weak answer, especially for a scientist. (My mother had been pre-med in college and had no room for superstition or faith of any kind. Her critiques of prejudice and sexism were based on a Kantian view of the relationship between experience and knowledge. Rationality and logic were everything to her and my father.) We debated for a while, and then I let it go.

Fast forward to 1995, fifty years later, and she's making a disparaging remark about religion. I ask her how she could have been an agnostic back in the fifties.

"I was never an agnostic," she protests.

"Yes you were," I counter. "Remember when we were discussing this back when I was in junior high? I distinctly remember your saying you were an agnostic!"

"Oh well, maybe I did say that, but that was because I was afraid that if I told you I was an atheist and you said that in public school, it would create problems for you. I don't think there were any people in Hampton at the time who were vocal about being atheists." (Her usual understatement.)

As the years passed, I read about the Holocaust and about anti-Semitism as part of my attempt to understand racism, which had shaped my life every day in the South. I told my Gentile friends that my family had lost relatives in the Holocaust, although I didn't know the names of anyone close. I imagined that second or third cousins of mine had died in the camps. When I was 65, I found out that a number of them had been rounded up, marched to large pits, shot, and buried in mass graves in the little towns of Burstyn and Rohatyn in Galicia. They still lie in those graves.

I occasionally light Hanukah lights. When my daughter was born, I began my own tradition of little presents every day of that winter holiday: "eight days of Hanukah, eight pairs of socks," we used to say. Gradually, I accepted attending some Kol Nidre services with one friend, I ate my share of *matzoh* at feminist and radical seders, and I became active in Palestinian-Israeli politics.

✦

It's 2004. I've just attended a prison health conference in Kiev, and am now visiting the small cities and towns where my relatives lived in the late 1800s.

I travel to Lvov and from there to three small towns nearby. In Burstyn, I see a gravestone with my mother's family name, Klarberg, in roman script, surrounded by other tumbled stones with writing in Hebrew or Yiddish. *How did that happen?* I wonder. My guides from the Jewish community in Lvov show me the mass graves of thousands of Jews in two other towns. This is the land of the Einsatzgruppen sweep of 1941. If I had lived there, I would have ended up in one of these weed-filled depressions or mounds, marked by small monuments placed by a recent Ukrainian government. Some of these graves have a second monument from Jews who came from the United States or Israel to erect them.

The second day of my trip to these family towns, I have a powerful visit in Rohatyn. It begins with looking at a meadow where Jewish men were forced to dig a large pit on the day the SS came. Then they and most of the Jewish women and children of the town were mowed down with guns and dumped in the pit. Now it's a site for agriculture. One can discern the outline of the pit by the higher reach of the corn growing there. There are two small monuments, one set up by Jews and another by Ukrainians. I notice that the last pink flowers of late summer are drying out around the border of the Jewish monument. Someone has tied them up with string so they lean toward the polished stone marker.

A local man comes up and asks what we're doing. Visiting

Jewish sites, my Lvov guides explain. The local tells us to go down the hill to meet the creator of an archive created in memory of the Jews who once constituted almost half of the town's population. Josef Kazinsky was eight at the time of the mass slaughter. His distressed father brought him to the gravesite we were just at in the evening after the shooting. Josef tells us that he could see the ground still moving from the last dying people under the dirt. He was so marked by the experience that he became a local historian. He taught for years about the Holocaust to students in the Rohatyn high school; he also set up an archive of documents about the Jews of Rohatyn. He gestures to a small stone building behind him where the archive is protected; he's the person who tends the memorials and their flowers in his town.

Josef shows us a former Jewish school, a three-story brick building, set in a large yard now used as part of the local town administration. He takes us to a tilted house surrounded by high grass. That's where the former rabbi lived; it's now home to a local family. One Jewish woman lives in the town, where previously there were about 4,000 Jews.

Then we drive with Josef in our Lvov car to the other side of Rohatyn, about 1 km, to what I've come to call The Garbage Dump Memorial. This was the most upsetting stop in my entire trip. In two mass shootings, first involving 2,000 people, and then about six months later, another shooting of 1,000 more, thousands were shot and buried in a connected set of graves on a small hillside. Josef says that the first to be killed were Jews; the later group included more Jews, political dissidents, and perhaps some Roma. The graves are now covered with a shrubby undergrowth of vines and brambles and mixed deciduous trees. Now, just in front of the graves, the town also has its trash dump. There are two memorials: one placed by Jews describing the dead (and tended by Josef through the year), the other placed by the Ukrainian government. The second memorial ignores any details about the people lying in the grave, describing them all as "Poles killed by the Germans." To the side of the memorials, a column of smoke rises from burning garbage.

How could anyone burn garbage on the site where 3,000 people were killed during the lifetime of the man standing next to me? And next to a double memorial to the dead? I just can't comprehend it. When I took the photograph below, I felt I had to record the scene because otherwise I might someday think I had imagined it. And I thought that others might not believe me when I told them what I had seen. This – and the cornfield, and the other mass graves of western Ukraine – are not big public monuments to the dead, like the concentration camps and the special sites for movies. They're not marked on maps. They are the detritus and the still-hidden reality of hundreds of thousands of deaths from the Anschluss of 1941. These are people who never made it to a concentration camp; they were just gunned down and almost haphazardly covered, not really even buried. Now others grow corn over them or burn garbage a few feet away.

I feel I learned more from this trip to western Ukraine than from any other trip in my life. I learned things I would rather not know about routinization of violence and killing and about the lack of caring afterward. And I discovered why my family had been so unwilling to talk about the past and the Holocaust. Maybe I was also looking at some of the deeper reasons my mother kept her atheism secret, and why my parents later listened so closely to the McCarthy hearings. The juxtaposition of burning garbage with the memorial to those who died left me with a sense that locals who kill their neighbors really can shut off feelings about the human beings who died. Now they just burn their garbage and turn away from the smell and the smoke.

CHAPTER 4

LEARNING TO ARGUE

t's 1956. I'm eating dinner with my family. We're sitting in our dining room, with its modern yellow and gray wallpaper. My parents had worked together to hang the rolls. I thought the resulting walls looked weird, so unlike those in any Alleghany Road or other Hampton homes I had been inside. Those homes held real – or imitation – antique furniture. They had flowered rugs, ruffled curtains, and indoor echoes of the outdoor magnolias on our street. If they had wallpaper, it would depict roses or realistic scenes, not abstract edgy yellow and gray leaves. Our dining room walls, however, were only one sign among many that my parents were Yankees. There was the dramatic music broadcast from the Metropolitan Opera direct to our radio every Saturday afternoon. Copies of *Scientific American* and the *Journal of the Institute of Electrical Engineering* were arranged on the coffee table. The reprints of paintings by Picasso, Miro, and Leger walked up the wall beside our stairs to the second floor. And a quartet of small watercolors of the Manhattan skyline decorated the east wall in the living room. We were foreigners in this land of my birth.

My parents may have bought the wallpaper nearby, but it was a New York style: based on early 20th-century modern paintings, and probably profiled in another of my mother's magazines, *Art News*. I could never understand why she read this journal. It seemed to be all about what was being shown at some New York galleries, where I knew she'd never go. Now I realize that our New York media, from the Sunday *Times* and *The New Yorker* to this very *Art News*, kept her grounded and helped her retain a different reference group than the Hampton reflected in the PTA at Armstrong Elementary School. I knew my friends would gawk at the wallpaper and the prints. So they did, but I think they liked being there, too. It was a touch of something different. And I knew from visiting their homes that it was a place of much greater freedom of thought, for them as well as us.

My mother had painted most of the rest of the house in locally acceptable, fairly mild, single colors. To my amazement, my father, the intellectual, had built a garage next to our house during weekends and on his days off in the summer. I have a photo of him putting on the roof shingles. So in some ways, our house was like those of our neighbors.

At dinnertime, we're all sitting around a rectangular dark wooden table on our stiff, high-backed chairs in the New York dining room. The tablecloth is a heavy white cotton with red and blue flowers. We use matching cloth napkins.

Mort sits with the window to the backyard behind him, in the one of the two chairs with arms. Ruth is at the other end in the matching armchair. Two chairs rest on each side. I sit with my back to the kitchen, one brother between me and my mother and the other brother directly across from me. The sixth chair is generally empty. On this day, things are peaceful among the three children. We know that if there is too much kicking under the table or bothering each other, our seating arrangements will be changed.

Preferred seating was always in a chair next to my father. I wonder now how my mother felt: did she thank her lucky stars she had an interesting husband, or did she feel less valued and secondary? For me, being in the single seat was like being an outcast. I would be too far away to whisper with one of my brothers when the grown-ups had their adult talk. Sitting next to my mother meant I was more likely to be asked to do an errand and less likely to monopolize my father's attention, even for a few minutes.

This is how we had every dinner in my youth, from the time we children were tall enough and skilled enough to sit at the dining table. It was always at the same time, even on the weekend, at 5:30 p.m. The time had been set to precisely half an hour after my father got home from work during the week. The format of dinner was also standardized. A meat, chicken, or fish dish, two vegetables, and a salad, followed by some kind of dessert. Usually there was also bread, butter, milk, and water on the table. Alcohol was never served.

As soon as my brothers and I could reach the kitchen counters and the tabletops, we were assigned tasks associated with the evening meal. By the time we were in the third grade, we had three rotating routines. One, set the table and make the salad. Two, wash all the dishes. And three, dry everything and put it away. Beginning in junior high, we did more tasks at the stove. In high school, when my mother was working full time, our collective job was to cook or heat up foods according to her extremely detailed directions and get everything else ready for both parents' arrival from their respective work locations. Every Monday, we rotated our dinner tasks. This was based on the (unwritten) Fairness Principles of Stoller Childrearing: "Take turns with everything, no privileges attached to gender or age."

At the table, every person served him or herself, with dishes moving in one direction around the table. We children were required to take, and eat, a minimum of three served spoonfuls of each food. Many times I found myself slowly chewing something I thought was terribly disgusting: liver with onions, oily mackerel, smelly asparagus. I was known as the family's "picky eater," a label I well deserved. My pickiness probably also contributed to my permanent skinniness.

On the other hand, we could take as much as we wished beyond that three-bite minimum, with the requirement that we finish whatever we took. Better to take a small amount and get seconds, which were almost always available, than to take too much and find oneself sitting at the table staring at a mound of string beans or a big piece of sweet potato that you had no room for. "No dessert until everything from the main course is gone from your plate." I think I learned these lessons pretty fast. (My parents were also quite consistent in their discipline, though they weren't mean or violent as far as I can remember.) Following the dinner rules, I internalized and transformed them into something that I thought of as part of "fairness" and "democracy" in eating.

As my friends still seem to find humorous, I also learned to eat salad at the end of the meal. Why do people think salad is an appetizer? To me, salad is the best part of every meal! If it came first all the time, I would probably not have any space for what most people think of as the main entrée and the supposed star of the meal. In addition, I thought, the main dishes were designed to be served hot, and if everyone – including the cook(s) – sat down at once, as they should (in my mind, this was another aspect of dinner democracy), how could the hot things still be the right temperature if we ate the salad first? I always thought eating salad after the main dishes was an eastern European tradition, or maybe something from Russia, because by family telling, it was the way of my father's family, and they were Russian. Maybe it was just a way to foreground the cooked meal and to also have us all together for the whole dinner. I don't think I'll ever know. I do know that, like most people, I thought my family way of eating was "normal" and that others who ate differently were a little strange.

When I wasn't staring unhappily at something I didn't want to eat, whispering, or kicking a brother, I was primarily looking in my father's direction. We usually all talked science, politics, technology, or a topic brought home from school. My father seemed to be the most knowledgeable about science. In chemistry and lab science, I'm sure my mother knew more, but my father was "the scientist" in our family hierarchy, and science was the highest value in our house.

It was during these dinners that I learned how to think critically. It certainly wasn't taught in my public school environment. Perhaps in the explicit "science" classes – biology, chemistry, and physics – we did learn to question and experiment. My chemistry teacher encouraged me to be a lawyer because I argued so much. (It was a compliment.) We also learned some logic in math, beginning in Algebra. Were we asked to think critically about history and politics in school? Could we ask our own questions about life in a literature class? Nope. We were supposed to accept what was in our texts, right or wrong, adding only what our teachers told us to. Memorize and repeat what's in the history book. Know the capitol cities of all the states. And be able to recite the names of all the characters as well as most of the text from *The Rime of the Ancient Mariner*. Ask serious questions about segregation or the Civil War? Absolutely not! Fortunately, at the Stoller dinner table, life was different.

We were challenged to think logically. No inferences were accepted without proof. We were taught how science worked, how research was done. I knew before I was out of high school about what different kinds of experiments there were, and what a control group was. I understood debates and how logic could be combined with evidence. I knew that if someone challenged one of my ideas, I had to be ready to answer that challenge with facts and logic. "Because I say so" was never an adequate answer in a discussion about the empirical world. Debate was encouraged as a way to test ideas, and to uncover prejudice or personal opinion masquerading as fact. We were taught that research and rational discussion were the way to test an idea. Emotions shouldn't be used to make a decision about real life actions with consequences. Everything, including emotions, could and should be discussed and studied before making a decision.

In the Stoller household, our discussions were called "arguments," as in "a scientific argument." They weren't "fights" as some people use the term "argument." Neither were they open-ended conversations, where people shared their opinions, experience, knowledge, and ideas in a general way. Most of them had a goal: to come up with an answer or answers to a complicated question. I thought they were lots of fun.

This evening, we happened to be discussing the question of why chess was so much more challenging than checkers. My father casually (I thought) suggested that all games are based on preparation for war. His model of the quintessential war preparation game was chess. It even had some obvious ingredients: knights, pawns, castles, bishops, kings, and queens. Chess was probably invented, he said, for kings to practice war strategies. This really piqued my attention and my desire to argue. I couldn't stand the idea that every time I played a game of chess – or Monopoly or softball – I was imitating war. (I must have already been some kind of pacifist.)

"Okay, so maybe chess is like war, but not softball," I said.

"Yes, it is. It's played to see who will win. Two teams, competition. There are strategies and tactics. Also, the players have to be in good physical condition. And the winner takes all."

"OK, how about Monopoly? Sometimes there are four players, not two armies!"

"Oh, it's still the same. Strategies, figuring out how to amass the most resources to win, sometimes making alliances."

This was only the first time we argued about the connection between games and war. I would lose the argument and then think up another point. Or I would try out another kind of game. Croquet? Solitaire? It seemed he could fit any game into his "preparation for war" argument. Finally, I just gave up and took his position in arguing this theory with others, hoping that someone would win against me so I could vanquish my father in a debate later.

Other times, we discussed the origin of the universe. We had long discussions about the Big Bang and other theories. Sometimes we ended with a question of importance to many Virginians: Is there any necessity for God? I must have asked this question ten or fifteen different ways, because it seemed that every friend I had believed that God made the universe. The issue of seven days from nothing to humans had not yet come to dominate school pedagogy. In fact, I don't remember ever hearing that the theory of evolution was a threat to the Southern way of life. In school, science and church were seen as two different spheres; science was done in a laboratory, and church told you how to live. The answer in our house to the question of God and the universe always ended with the same conclusion: no God needed. Another entity would be superfluous. As Stephen Hawking said later, "One can't prove that God doesn't exist, but science makes God unnecessary."

We discussed prejudice many times, often during dinner. My parents both believed, or at least told us they believed, that prejudice is the result of ignorance. This simply didn't seem true to me. Wythe Holt, who sat next to me in many of my junior high classes, convinced me that my parents were wrong on this point. Wythe was the smartest boy I knew and was also totally racist. He didn't seem to be the least bit ignorant, but I couldn't get him to change his mind at all about his idea that black people just weren't as smart as whites and were more dangerous. Of course, some "big thinkers" (take Arthur Jensen and William Shockley, for example) were just as convinced as Wythe was about black inferiority. So why was I surprised that Wythe thought white people were smarter than anyone else?

I didn't win the "ignorance causes prejudice" debate with my parents, but I knew I was onto something that they didn't get. I eventually concluded that the racist has a different standard for judging facts than the anti-racist does. In racialized thinking, there *are* races. In non-racial thinking, there aren't. The way we examine any assertions about "race" is deeply affected by whether we hold to a frame that race has an essence. Similarly, if we believe there's only one "truth" we examine arguments differently than if we believe there are multiple truths.

I grew to believe that both knowledge and standards of truth are socially constructed. My parents, wedded to science and a positivist view of knowledge, believed that there were definitive facts. Real proof required evidence and logical argument. While this training was part of my general introduction to critical and scientific thinking, it occurred especially in the context of understanding and challenging stereotypes, prejudice, and racism. So from the very start, I saw debate and the development of ideas as activities informed by social values. This was the basic lesson about knowledge that has shaped my entire life in terms of my curiosities, studying, teaching, and politics.

Ruth and Mort's fact: "In 1955, Negroes don't vote in Hampton, Virginia, because they are prevented by the poll tax and the sheriff."

If Wythe couldn't prove that Negroes were "just too lazy to vote," then to Mort and Ruth, he was just ignorant of the true facts. They were sure that if he knew the truth, he wouldn't say Negroes were too lazy. I knew, though, that his racism wasn't susceptible to these facts. It was part of his basic framing of reality, learned as a child and reinforced every day in our segregated city and state. Unless his framing changed, no amount of "facts" really mattered. And to him, any fact could be interpreted through his racist frame. My frame – and that of my parents – was one that began with the assumption that there were no "races" in human nature and that "racial difference" in behavior had to be explained by other causes. Wythe and I brought different views of the world and different assumptions about knowledge and logic to the most basic questions of race relations.

In college, I was taught the phrase "philosophical argument." A philosophical argument was examined for its assumptions, its content, and its logic. To me, this was something different from a "debate." I think of debates as competitive and ultimately inconclusive. I never wanted to be part of a debate club: too stressful, too intense, too formalized, and too focused on winning instead of discovery. I've always been drawn instead to people who like to argue about topics. What is prejudice? What is more important: following the law or our own sense of truth and ethics? When should my sense of truth take priority over another person's sense of truth? These discussions and arguments can be as mundane as "what is the best route to the next city on our cross-country journey?" or "when should tulips be planted?" I still love the learning I get from discussing them.

In high school I managed to get in trouble both at school and at home by challenging content, assumptions, and logic in arguments. My at-home failures usually had this form: if Mary

Beth can stay out until midnight, why can't I? And my school failures looked like this: If black people constitute 50% of the city of Newport News, why do they only get 10% of the school budget? Even when I lost, I loved the process of the argument.

My friend Helen Longino calls our dinner table type of discussion "critical interaction" or "critical discursive interaction." I realized after talking with her recently that my brothers and I were being taught what is now popularly described as "critical thinking." It was the opposite of what we were generally taught in the white public schools of Hampton and Newport News. There, the textbooks and the teachers were always the ultimate authority. We were taught "uncritical thinking." I suppose we could call *that* a skill too, useful for keeping your head down before an authoritarian government.

To me, any topic can be enjoyed through argument. How do we understand the changes in our world? What is a non-judgmental way of looking at them? I know we won't have a definitive answer, but I want to hear what other people think. I also want to try out my own ideas. I want to understand all aspects of the discussion as best I can at this moment in time. My feelings about it might also change. If I understand the changes, I'm sure my opinions from before we started talking will change, and I'll have new ideas about how to relate to the 21st-century world that I am now living in. It's all about learning what's going on around us.

There was a straight line from these early discussions at the dinner table to my choice of major in college: Philosophy. I think I chose that major for two reasons. First there was the appeal of argument and logic and the goal of "truth." Growing up in the racist thinking of the segregated south and what I saw as Southern non-logic, I yearned to be able to out-argue the Southern thought, racism, and prejudice that lay behind the weird culture of my youth. Secondly, I liked the idea that I was studying the "hardest" major, which in my 17-year-old mind made me like my father, who I thought was the smartest person in my family. I had also heard he was "one of the smartest people in NACA/NASA." He actually *was* a rocket scientist. I knew I wasn't going to be a rocket scientist myself, since physics and I did not speak the same language. I did want to be able to figure out some of the basic questions of how both the universe, and more closely, humans worked. Why do sane people have gaps in logic and argument? I wanted to know how to uncover those gaps and show them the truth: for instance, of equality. I wanted to know "can a smart person be a racist?" "How could a German believe that it made sense to kill all the Jews?" (I didn't know about Rohatyn then, but it's still the same question.) And of course, I was sure that my own opinions and assumptions were correct.

Those dinner discussions also turned my head to the direction that led to my college minor, Sociology, with its search for empirical data to help answer questions about the world I was living in. While in college, this desire to know the social context of truth increasingly intertwined with both my experiences in the civil rights movement and my growing desire to understand the Holocaust.

At 37 Alleghany Rd, after dinner, we each went a different way within the house, usually to read, or for us youth, to finish our homework. It was quiet; my father would be in his regular armchair, with a footstool stacked with papers and files from work. My mother would be puttering in the kitchen or reading a magazine. (I now realize how sexist and dismissive the term "puttering" is of the work she was actually doing.) By 1957, we had a small black and white TV, on which the whole family watched a program or two together some evenings. And there were always magazines and bookcases of books.

When we were small, my mother took us to the library

weekly (whites only at that library), where each child had a card. I loved the library and eventually rode my bike to the one in Hampton, or took the bus to the library in Newport News. My first regular paying job, in the tenth grade, was as a library assistant in the Newport News Public Library, where I "read the shelves" and made sure that all the books were in order.

CHAPTER 5

WHAT IT'S LIKE:
RACISM IN HAMPTON

When my parents arrived in Hampton in 1939, the global economic depression remained powerful. The war in Europe, which would create so many jobs and kill so many of my extended family, was already underway. In Europe, the rise of the Nazis and the growing demonization of Jews had already produced *Kristallnacht*; the complete exclusion of Jewish students from schools in Germany in 1938; a pogrom that sent 30,000 Jews to Dachau, Buchenwald, and Sachsenhausen; and the flight of 340,000 Jews from Germany and Austria.

While New York Jews like my parents were probably aware of these developments in the late 1930s, I think that Mort and Ruth felt safe and somewhat removed because all their close relatives had left Europe before 1900. Still, as I was growing up, they repeatedly told me that the reasons for their own parents' departures from Eastern Europe were to escape pogroms in their hometowns. Whether it was in Poland or Russia, "It was all the same if you were Jewish." One thing I always knew: I was

NOT a Pole or a Russian. I was a Jew, born a Jew, and destined to be one throughout my life. It had nothing to do with whether I was religious. It was a label that would always be a part of me. In the nineteenth century, I was told, a Jew could live safely in Eastern Europe or Russia for a while, and then there would be a pogrom. I later discovered that between 1880 and 1924, over 2 million Jews left Europe for the United States and South America to escape pogroms. Each of my grandparents came by a different trajectory, but all four had arrived as children by the early 20th century. And all four came after one pogrom or another.

Perhaps it was what they knew as Jews, about stereotyping, violence, and genocide, that made my parents so definite in their stand against segregation. They were a lot more progressive than any of our New York relatives. My Klarberg cousins and their parents said prejudiced things about African Americans; they also said surprisingly hostile things about other people who weren't Jewish. Italians were "fat" and "in the Mafia"; the Irish "drank a lot" and were fated to be alcoholics. My parents opposed prejudice and stereotyping of any group. So their opposition to segregation couldn't be just because they came from New York, where there was no legally required segregation.

I think they also may have been drawn to this more open way of thinking because of their shared faith in science and rationalism. They both rejected the ways of "the old country" and embraced liberalism and democracy. My mother even refused to have her ears pierced because it was "old-fashioned." Only in the 1970s, when it was hard to find earrings with screw or clip-on findings, did she accede to this style. Meanwhile, my father happily freed his two sons from the bar mitzvah ritual. Both parents were science majors in college and lifelong atheists.

There was a copy of Marx's *Capital* in my father's bookshelf, one of only three or four non-fiction works that were not about engineering, astronomy, or physics. Several members of my father's engineering cohort of 1938 were later interrogated by HUAC and Joseph McCarthy in the 1950s. We listened to the hearings on the radio at dinner and our parents were unusually quiet. The presence of *Das Kapital* was an important sign of how different my parents were from other Virginians I knew – even though as a child, I had no idea who Marx was. Perhaps reading Marx was as deviant as being an atheist, and therefore better left undiscussed with three young children who were already being encouraged to share their radical opinions on race with friends or strangers when faced with segregationist "malarkey."

Our education about equality had always included sharing all chores equally among the children: no boy's chores vs. girl's chores. As we got old enough, we each cleaned our rooms every Saturday morning, and every week we were taking turns with the tasks associated with dinner. Outdoors work was also rotated: mowing the lawn, clipping the hedges, sweeping the sidewalk. My mother was an early feminist. I remember her telling me proudly that women got the right to vote during the year she was born. She didn't take credit for it, of course, but it seemed to reinforce her commitment to participating in the electoral process and policy-making. For my father, democracy and equality were corollaries of rational thinking.

In mid-20th century Virginia, the segregation of public institutions was required by law. Both a poll tax and a voting test excluded blacks from registering. All county and city governments were in the hands of whites, regardless of the demographics of the municipality. Marriages between white and black were illegal, and remained so until 1968. Deference was required everywhere: In Hampton, if a white person got on a bus, black people were required to move back, so that no black person could sit, even in an otherwise empty row, forward of any white person. From my early childhood, I learned to sit as far forward as possible, so as not to disturb any black riders already on the bus.

My earliest memories of racism concern learning how to talk correctly. No one could use the word "nigger" at our house or around my parents. "Nigra" was equally unacceptable, since it was how middle and upper-class whites showed their racism while avoiding saying "nigger." If a friend of mine was over and used either of those words, it was my job to immediately explain that they would have to go home if they said it again. I knew it was my responsibility to be sure that my parents did not hear those words from me or from my friends.

I also knew to give advance warning to my friends who came from prejudiced families. I would wait until we were on the sidewalk in front of our house and had just turned toward our front porch. "I just want you to know that you can't say anything bad about Negroes in our house, and no one, not even an adult, is allowed to say 'nigra.' Otherwise, my parents are completely normal." I was afraid if I explained earlier than the front yard, they might think my parents were too weird and not come over at all. With one foot on the first step, they always just came on in. Occasionally, one of my parents would have to remind someone who was already at play in the living room or seated at the dining table. I remember it being done in a gentle, informative way: "We don't talk that way here…" Everyone adjusted easily, as far as I remember.

My parents made it clear that no one was "born prejudiced." They told us, no doubt at one of those dinner discussions, that prejudice was something that many other parents in the South taught their children. "And where did *they* get it from?" we wanted to know. "Their parents."

◆

Nancy: "Why did Ray Womble say that Negroes carried knives and that was why they had to sit in the back of the bus?"

Mort: "He's just ignorant. He doesn't know any better. Just ask him if he's ever seen a Negro on the bus with a knife, and if he says yes, be prepared that 'he might just be saying that.'"

✦

"You're just saying that" was a common expression in Hampton, meaning "there's no factual basis for your comment." In other words, Ray might have "just been saying that" to support his point.

Mort: "And you ask him if whites don't also carry knives, too."

This was one way I was taught that any assertion about race needed to be proved. If it wasn't proved, I could treat it as just that: someone's personal assertion. It was an opinion, not a fact.

According to both my parents, a person could either be taught to think clearly or he could be told a lot of prejudiced things and learn a lot of stereotypes. This is the dichotomy we were brought up with. On the one side, ours, there was rationality, education, tolerance, and equality for all. On the other side there was ignorance, prejudice, stereotypes, and support of segregation. I don't think that I ever doubted that our way was right, but I was aware that almost every one of my friends and probably all of their parents had very different ideas than were espoused in my family.

We called supporters of the southern system of white privilege segregationists, not racists. I was also taught a set of concepts that distinguished prejudice, stereotypes, discrimination, and acquiescence to local norms from "true" racism. The last term was saved for the more vicious and violent extremists, and those who openly supported physical attacks on black people. One might debate whether a member of the White Citizens Council was simply (!) a segregationist or a "true" racist; but there was no debate about a member of the Ku Klux Klan. I was taught that members of the KKK hated black people and that they would harm whites as well if they sided with Negroes. Although the Klan was not active in our town, as far as I knew, there was an undercurrent of fear even in the white world about the violence that could be perpetrated on Negroes or on their supporters. And I was well aware that, as Jews, we could also face the stone wall of prejudice and exclusion.

In the third grade, after three blissful years at the wonderful private Robert Sugden School, I discovered definitively that public schools were the main location outside the home where local children were taught the language and acceptance of racism. Whether it was from a teacher or a text, all history was told from a white perspective. The only somewhat sympathetic message about Negroes was this: "They were slaves, but that was long ago." It was *so long ago*, as far as we knew from our teachers, that we didn't need to hear anything specific about it. The story of the daily lives of slaves was told in a few bland paragraphs, while the story of white people before the Civil War required many books and years of study. My main impression was that slaves "came" from Africa, they worked in agriculture on plantations in the deeper South, they lived in small wooden cabins, and that as a style of dress, the women tied their hair up in bandannas.

When I first entered public school in 1949, there were surely people in Hampton who had lived as slaves. Slavery had ended in 1865, only 74 years before. Undoubtedly there were hundreds or even thousands of the 8,000 African Americans in our county, or of the 20,000 African Americans living in the city of Newport News where I went to high school, whose *parents* had been slaves. Our classes repeatedly taught the white experience of the Civil War as recent history. The black experience of slavery remained remote and foreign, as if it had occurred in another country altogether. Teachers and texts mentioned

Reconstruction as a brief period of northern (not even federal) interference in Southern politics. It hadn't worked out because of the "carpetbaggers." They ignored the development of the Jim Crow South. The term "Jim Crow" was used descriptively, sometimes informally outside of school, but it never appeared in any of my textbooks.

The lives of contemporary African Americans anywhere in the United States, including in our own town, never appeared in any curriculum. Like every other public institution in Virginia, the school system was completely segregated socially as well as intellectually. I don't believe I ever saw an African American in any public school I attended, even working as a janitor. Thirty percent of the population of Hampton was black. Newport News was almost half black. One of the most important Freedman's Bureau colleges, Hampton Institute (now Hampton University), formerly run by Booker T. Washington, was located in my hometown. In public school, on the radio, or in the newspaper, we heard nothing about black life or a black college in our town. If my parents hadn't taken us to concerts at Hampton Institute, we might never have been on the campus at all, but merely bicycled or driven by and seen only trees, grass, and some red brick buildings in the shade.

However, Virginia's important food industries of tobacco, oysters, and crabbing relied heavily on black labor. Tobacco sowing, transplanting, weeding, and harvesting were the jobs of excruciatingly poor black sharecroppers, even in the 1940s and '50s. Later, in 1962, I met some of these sharecroppers while working in a Freedom Center in Prince Edward County. As a white child and teenager, I only knew that tobacco was a big industry in Virginia. Plantations were represented as beautiful houses on manicured lawns with old "slave houses" from centuries past. The old slave houses weren't seen as places where men, women, and children, owned by others, lived in last century, or 90 years ago, if we count back to 1865 from 1955 when I entered high school, but "centuries" ago.

African Americans cleaned and packed crabs at the smelly crab factory in downtown Hampton. They shucked the oysters that were the number one export from the Chesapeake Bay until the late 1970s. Our (white) high school mascot was the Chesapeake Bay Blue Crab. We were the Hampton Crabbers, and we showed it to everyone with a large white chenille crab stitched on the back of each red and white varsity letter jacket. Whites owned the crab processing companies, just as they owned and managed all the major industries in the area. So it was easy for whites to think of the crabs as "ours," i.e., the property of white people, because in a way, they were, even if they had once lived independent lives at the bottom of Hampton Roads.

I was in junior high when US Supreme Court issued its decision in Brown v. Board of Education, invalidating all school segregation as "inherently unequal." The next day, Mr. Howard, my social studies teacher, informed us of the decision. Mentioning an actual political event was rare in our class. His message, however, was striking: "Don't worry," he informed us, "desegregation won't come to our schools for a long, long time. I can promise you that it won't be in my lifetime or yours of being in school. It will be after I retire and long after you graduate, if it ever comes." I was sure that he was wrong, which just shows how little my social studies classes had taught me. I had a magical view of the US Supreme Court, which was not surprising, given the schematic education I had about US government. I thought that if the Supreme Court made a decision, it immediately changed how things were done. We lived in a land of law and the Court was the final arbiter of those laws. Ipso facto—it's done. How little I knew!

Virginia became the leader of the southern "massive resistance" strategy after the Brown decision. Schools in Hampton, where I had attended elementary and junior high, finally deseg-regated in 1963, nine years after the ruling and six years after I left. In Newport News, where I attended high school, it took until 1971, a full seventeen years and a lot of work after the rul-ing, until blacks and whites were studying together. By then it was twelve years after I had graduated from the school, so my teacher was actually correct.

Although I had been an A student in 1954, I had little preparation for the Supreme Court announcement. Our Social Studies classes had been limited to teaching us about the three branches of government: legislative, judicial, and executive. We also knew that there were local, state, and federal governments. We even had a rudimentary idea about when each system had originated historically. After all, we had been told that Virgin-ian history and American history were the almost the same for us, with precedence given to the Virginia narrative. We had heard from first grade onward about the settlement of the col-onies, and knew how Pocahontas had saved the life of Captain John Smith, right in our hometown of Hampton.

We had been taught that all these systems had developed through struggle against the British crown. They had evolved in a godly harmony. Power and conflict (beyond the Revolu-tionary War and other wars at a national level), much less seg-regation, had never been discussed in school. We did know that slavery had once existed, but it was something that ended as a result of the Civil War, and that, we were reminded, was almost a hundred years ago. To me, a hundred years ago seemed like another country, with people dressed in strange clothes that might have been worn a thousand years ago. If white and black were discussed in class, it was to say that we lived in peace, as long as we didn't have to live too close together.

Because my family was from the North, and because I vis-ited New York every summer, I knew that there were places where white and black shared bus seats and went to the same schools; they even sat in the same classrooms. And I knew that my parents thought that was how we should be living.

So when Mr. Howard announced the court decision and told us not to worry, I was confused, anxious, and afraid. Confusion bloomed because I knew nothing about this Supreme Court decision, or how something decided by a national court could affect our school system down here in Tidewater Virginia. I was also confused about how any court ruling could take years to take effect. I always imagined that every decision would be immediately carried out. When a court convicts a burglar, he is taken away immediately; why wouldn't it happen like that in our schools?

While I was sitting in that classroom, my confusion soon gave way to anxiety. Mr. Howard was reassuring us. Why was reassurance necessary? I wondered. It seemed that some bad thing was imminent, but we shouldn't worry, as it wouldn't actually happen. Who would prevent *it*? And were we forbidden to be actors or even observers in this drama that we did not understand, but was at the same time all about us? It was after all *our* current and future school experiences that he was talking about.

And then there was fear. I wanted to ask why we should be so afraid. It was clear that this was a basic assumption not to be challenged. Mr. Howard spoke as if he were channeling the common view within our classroom, among our teachers and parents and in the school system. This view was: of course we wouldn't want to go to school with black children. That was unquestionable. I did, however, want to voice some question. At the same time, I felt I knew nothing about the lawsuit, the court, or how schools could change their demographics. What could I say without challenging my teacher in a way that was doomed to fail? I had to say something during this out-of-the-ordinary moment. The best question I found to ask was, "Why do you think it will be so long before the schools are desegregated?"

"Because Virginia won't let it happen," he said. That didn't really tell me much, but it silenced me. No one else said anything.

In the fall of 1958, four years after the *Brown* decision, when I entered my senior year at Newport News High School, six white seniors from the nearby city of Norfolk, just across Hampton Roads, attended our classes. When their own school board had refused to desegregate, a federal judge had ordered the school system completely shut unless opened to all fairly. The Norfolk school board had closed the entire school system for a year, but these students' parents wanted them to graduate from some high school soon and go to college. They made a deal with our school district to let their children attend for a year. Interestingly, the students were all Jewish (which increased the Jewish population of my class cohort from four to ten, out of 180 students). They came by carpool every day. I was fascinated. Racial politics had begun to have an impact on our school.

In addition to critiquing the local culture of segregation, my parents were quietly active in breaking its rules. When we went to concerts at Hampton Institute, we were among a small minority of white attendees, perhaps twenty or thirty people out of an audience of 300. Sitting with courteous and well-dressed men, women, and children listening to symphonies that could be heard nowhere else in our town influenced my view of black people.

My mother and Margaret Harrison, the wife of the Episcopal minister of the most prominent white church in town, were leaders of the white (all female) activists who were part of the desegregation of the Girl Scout Council and the League of Women Voters, a national organization advocating for women to vote and for fair voting practices. According to our family lore, in both cases my mother was the first white woman to get involved. She told us that she could never have done it without the support of someone in an "old Southern family." Margaret's husband was descended from signers of both the Declaration of Independence and the Constitution. Margaret was the liberal in that household. She brought Chicago money and her own liberalism to the highly respectable but less than wealthy family. I knew their children, and I knew that they retained more of their father's racial politics than hers. However, as teenagers they did at least complain when they found out that my brothers and I couldn't go with them to the Hampton Yacht Club, about a block from their home. (Why not? Because we were Jewish.) So Ruth recruited Margaret to both ventures. I think they must have met in the League of Women Voters.

As my mother tells the League story, one day she was sitting in one of their meetings when she noticed there were no Negro women in the room. "Isn't this supposed to be the League of Women Voters? Not the League of White Women Voters?" she said.

Others agreed. And so they began a process of reaching out to Black women. And from then on, the League was mixed.

With the Girl Scouts, desegregation began at the Girl Scout Council level. The national organization of Scouting had already authorized integrated troops. There was a black Girl Scout troop in Hampton, but without access to the resources of the white council, which helped support several white troops. At the time that I was an active Scout, Ruth was on the Council and pushed for the change, along with Margaret's help. I don't know the details, but it must have been successful, because when I went to the first Girl Scout Roundup in 1956, we included a black scout in our patrol.

We had the only integrated patrol from anywhere in Virginia. My troop leader, Helen Mulcahay, who accompanied our patrol to the Michigan Roundup, was also instrumental in helping one of the African American "computers" (memorialized in the book and film *Hidden Figures*) to prepare for her trip to a national Girl Scout leadership conference held soon after in the Rocky Mountains.

This desegregation of the Girl Scouts and the League of Women Voters couldn't have happened without the work of African Americans in Hampton. I never heard about their roles. And I didn't even know my own mother's role in either change until she told me some years later. My own white nearsightedness and family focus made me unaware for a long time of my oversights in not asking more about how it all happened. I never asked my mother, and now she and the others are all dead.

One fall day in my senior English class, we were given an extra credit option to write an essay for a local Chamber of Commerce contest. I decided to enter, since I wanted all the A's I could get. The topic was "My True Security: The American Way." The local winner would get $100 and their paper entered in a statewide competition. My essay stressed that there were a lot of problems in the United States, but that the good thing about living here was that one could try to change it. I was thinking completely about segregation, and although my paper didn't say words like Negro and white, they were in the meaning of every sentence. I'm not sure if there were even other essays submitted from my high school, but mine was forwarded to the Chamber of Commerce and then won the county competition. The youth page of the local newspaper featured my accomplishment and my essay advanced to the next level. At the state contest, I came in second. I was a little embarrassed that my work, which discussed how flawed the United States was, could be acceptable to a mainstream institution. Was I a hypocrite? Perhaps this was what the business community wanted to hear from idealistic teenagers: their faith that nothing radical needed to happen. Was I saying that all the change we needed was the slow progress of the present?

My prize was a new *Encyclopedia Americana*. Now what would I do with that? I was about to go to college, where I knew I wouldn't need it. After a conversation with my parents, I sold it for $150, took my winnings, and bought a bus ticket to Tucson to see my old friend Gene Mercer. She had been living there with her (now divorced) mother for the past two years. I spent my transitional summer between high school and college discovering coffee houses, folk music, the desert, and the joys of minimal adult supervision. I knew I was about to say goodbye to the narrow thinking of Hampton, Virginia, and that my life was about to open up in new and unimaginable ways. I thought I was leaving the segregated South behind.

PART II

SOUTHERN YANKEE IN

THE DIXIE COURT

CHAPTER 6

BOWLING FOR FREEDOM

On October 4, 1957, while I was still in the 11th grade and doing my best to get B's or better in solid geometry and chemistry, the Soviet Union launched Sputnik, the first satellite to orbit the earth. This far-away event was the beginning of a major change for my family, leading to a new home and a new state to live in. At the same time, it created my direct route into the sit-in movement.

Following Sputnik, my father's employer, the National Advisory Committee on Aeronautics, morphed into the National Aeronautics and Space Administration. By October 1958, a year after Sputnik, the new agency was ready to function. Mort was appointed NASA's Chief of Space Science. He began spending most of his work week in Washington at the expanded national headquarters. Since my brothers and I had just entered our senior year of high school, our parents decided that we should finish where we were. The full family would move to DC to join Mort in the summer of 1959, as soon after graduation as possible.

Ruth was determined to leave segregated Virginia. Since

she was in charge of house hunting, the only houses she was willing to consider had to be in either the District of Columbia or Montgomery County, known then to be the more liberal of the two Maryland counties edging the District to the north. By mid-summer of 1959, our house on Alleghany Rd. had been sold (to a Black family, the first to be able to buy a home on our block) and our new home (gently pre-used) was ready for us in the liberal neighborhood of Bannockburn, in the southeast corner of Montgomery County. During the actual move, I was off in Tucson drinking coffee and listening to folk music. When I arrived in August, staying only a few weeks before going off to college, I saw that our house was just a half-mile from the Glen Echo Amusement Park. The park was a whites-only segregated establishment, but I don't think that made much of an impression on me. I know I didn't visit it. I was too busy getting ready to leave for Massachusetts. And I didn't know then how much the geographic proximity between our house and the Park would alter the details and the direction of my life. First I had to go further north. I was about to set the pattern of my life for the next six years: north, mid-south, further south; repeat; repeat again.

By early September, I was a first-year student at Wellesley College, an elite women's school in a suburb of Boston. I thought Wellesley would provide a welcome change from the segregated environment of my childhood. Encouraged by my mother, I believed that I had to leave Virginia to get a different view and live a different life. I had other choices for college, including the liberal Oberlin and the big city Barnard. I wanted to become as smart and critical as possible. I had heard that this college was the most academically challenging, even if it was kind of fancy. And the idea of living in New York City would put me to close to my relatives, and in the midst of a lot of noise. So Wellesley it would be.

Wellesley, however, turned out to be virtually all white, with quotas set for both black and Jewish students. There were many more Jews than blacks in my cohort, though there were many more blacks living in the United States than Jews. I could see the reality of the black quota easily: there were no more than four or five black students in our first year group of 500. Perhaps one percent of the cohort. Even today, there are three times as many international students at Wellesley and twice as many Asian/Pacific Islanders as African Americans, who comprised seven percent of the Class of 2019 (but fourteen percent of the US population).

It was not until sometime in the 1980s that I discovered that I myself had been part of the Jewish quota. (I was so used to being one of very few Jews in my hometown that being surrounded by Gentiles seemed completely normal.) My class of 1963 was also filled with wealthy debutantes and private school graduates. Those who had any politics at all seemed to be conservative Republicans. During my first week, I was already wondering how I would survive socially, even if I passed all my courses.

I knew my high school education was poor compared to most of the other students, but I tried to settle into the alien environment. I signed up for my first philosophy course, got put in beginning French despite two years of high school study, and was sent to a speech class to correct my Southern accent. I refused the last assignment. That was really insulting! To have an extra-curricular activity, I joined the campus newspaper staff, even though I seemed to be studying in every spare moment just to understand how college worked. I was often lost on the 500-acre campus and sometimes wondered if I could even find my way back to my dormitory before dinner. When the winter set in, I froze in my southern winter coat. It took me two years to discover that most students wore long underwear and heavy wool socks. My own idea of a winter coat was their idea of something to wear just before Easter.

Four months after my arrival, in early February of 1960, I saw that the *Boston Globe* had reported the beginning of a "sit-in" movement at a Woolworth's Five and Dime Store in Greensboro, North Carolina. African American college students were refusing to leave the segregated lunch counter unless they were served. Denied service, they "sat in" and waited until the store closed. Returning the next day and the next, for two weeks, their numbers grew to 300 supporters. Their movement spread in North Carolina and throughout the South, where Woolworth's had many of its 2,500 American stores. Lunch counters were important customer draws in many of these stores, and thus provided an easy base for the spread of this activist approach to the desegregation of public space. Within several months, the Greensboro sit-ins succeeded, and the movement they spawned created the direct action side of the 1960s civil rights movement.

In Boston, the mid-February television news covered the Greensboro sit-ins and similar actions elsewhere in the South. Within two weeks, a spontaneous direct action support movement had begun in the North. The northern, leaderless, youth-led movement featured sympathy pickets of Woolworth's Five and Dime stores. This tactic of opposing segregation in a public space appealed to me. It was something I would have liked to do back home in Hampton, but I had never known it was possible. And there was a Woolworth's directly across from the front gate of Wellesley College. This was irresistible! I rounded up three other staff members from the paper. We made some picket signs with slogans copied from what we'd seen in the news. The next day at lunchtime, we crossed through the Wellesley gate to the other side of Main Street and the local Woolworth's store. Both our sympathy picket and my direct action career began that day.

Within an hour, word of our picketing had gotten back to the college administration. Someone from the Dean of Students' office came over to tell us to stop. We took our time. The next morning, we each received a phone call telling us to come to the Dean's Office. If we wanted to address discrimination, said the Dean, we should do it on campus. We shouldn't disturb the locals or ruin the good relations between the college and the town. And would we please wear long coats over our blue jeans or else put on skirts if did go out there? The clear message was to keep our activism on campus.

We did start an on-campus civil rights group, but we also kept on picketing for another week. Our on-campus group then identified various problems at the college: discrimination in local guesthouse policies, the incredibly poor acceptance rate for black students, the lack of black professors. We directed some, but only some, of our attention toward these issues. We also used our organization as a springboard for students who wished to link to the broader movement.

I was incredibly happy. After six months at Wellesley, I had found something that generated a passion, almost an obsession. At seventeen, I had become a local activist and the prime organizer of the Wellesley College Civil Rights Group. I had friends, a purpose, and I felt linked to a growing network of like-minded people spread around the country. I was publicly opposing and refusing to cooperate with segregation, an institutional system that had organized every part of my youth, a system my parents had described as perhaps the worst evil in our society. Now I had entered an interracial world. I could talk seriously and casually to black people my age who had grown up in a world that was interwoven with mine, but which I had seen only from the corner of my eye for seventeen years. Our small but committed civil rights group remained active as long as I was at Wellesley. After I had graduated, when the college finally began to admit more African American students, they took leadership of subsequent groups.

At the beginning of the summer of 1960, I spent six stressful weeks in New York City, living with one and then the other of my father's aunts while I attended summer school at Columbia to advance in the social science curriculum back at Wellesley. On my return to Bannockburn in mid-July, I discovered a picket line at the segregated Glen Echo Amusement Park. The D.C Area Non-violent Action Group (DC NAG) organized it to protest the exclusion of blacks from the park. For the rest of the summer, I went there to picket every afternoon.

The picket line and the people I met there became my life, my friendship circle, my reference group, and my future community of radicals. Within days, I was participating in sit-ins at other locations in Maryland with NAG members and volunteers. We were especially active in suburban Maryland, often traveling to a restaurant or other public space after our picket line ended at nine or ten in the evening – either for recreation or, if necessary, to desegregate the place.

One evening in September, 1960, we decided to go bowling. Someone had heard of a beautiful new bowling alley with the enticing name of Fair Lanes. It was in the suburbs, not too far but over the county line in Prince Georges, which had a reputation for being much more brutal to those who challenged segregation. No one had heard of African Americans bowling at Fair Lanes, but we didn't think it had ever been tested. This was the Upper South, where some places were accessible while others were not.

We arrived around 10 p.m., maybe six or seven of us in two cars, half white and half black, with two or three women and four or five men. We were all college age except for Paul Dietrich, a white man of about 30, who most of us thought to be a communist. (Actually, he was a former seminary student who joined the Freedom Riders and worked with the poor for years.) We were in two cars. I went in with one white guy, perhaps Paul, to rent the shoes so we would have a better chance of bowling. Then the black members of our group joined us at two lanes in the center of the alley. We all immediately put on our shoes and started to play. None of the bowlers near us seemed to notice anything. We were elated. We had desegregated the place just like that! Then one of our group noticed a discussion at the shoe rental desk. A young man came over and told us we had to leave.

"I'm sorry," he said politely, "this place is for whites only."

A member of our group responded that we didn't seem to be creating any problems; we had just come to bowl, and the other clients didn't care. He told us that we were making a disturbance. One of us responded that it was *he* who was making the disturbance. It went like that for a few minutes, after which he informed us that he would have to call the police. Okay, we responded, and went back to bowling. As did all the other bowlers.

About ten minutes later, the police arrived. In my memory there were four or five of them: all white, of course. They were Prince Georges County Sheriff's Department deputies. After a short conversation at the shoe counter, during which the desk clerk pointed to us, they came to our lanes and told us to leave or be arrested. Of course we declined to leave. They began pulling us, one after the other, from the alleys. Our plan was to delay as much as possible, while their plan was to move us out as quickly as they could.

"What about my shoes?" someone asked.

"Okay, you can take them off."

After all, why should the bowling alley lose seven pairs of shoes? We each sat down and, in slow motion, unlaced our bowling shoes and methodically found our street shoes to put them on. We took our time on our purpose, but the deputies began pulling the men in our group out the door in their stocking feet. My job was to collect and return the bowling shoes – slowly, very slowly. Meanwhile, no one at Fair Lanes was bowling. They all watched as the police handcuffed us and "encouraged" us to leave. The deputies became increasingly agitated. Finally, the evident protection I had as a young white woman came to an abrupt end; a cop extended his arm, pushed up rapidly under my hands, and sent seven pairs of shoes flying into the air. Even though it was violent and shocking, something about the scene felt exhilarating, even funny.

Outside the men were being put in the backs of the police cars. Paul gave me his car keys.

"Follow us to the jail!"

Paul's car had a stick shift. I had learned to drive a stick shift three years earlier, but I'd never driven Paul's car. I was so nervous that I could barely back out of my parking space. We formed a caravan: first the two police cars with all the men in them, then our two movement cars, driven by the women. My vehicle was second, and I was in it alone. Another sheriff's car followed me. The deputy behind me drove closer and closer, then turned on his red and blue lights. I was terrified. My left foot shook so hard on the clutch that I thought I wouldn't be able to come to a smooth stop.

"Yes?" I asked.

"Your license plate light is not bright enough. Give me your driver's license and the car registration."

I was alone with the police on a dark road.

I found the registration and license, waited for my ticket, and then followed the highway to the jail, still driving slowly and nervously with the cop behind me. After finding out the price of bail and calling our lawyer, I drove Paul's car to my home and returned to the jail the next morning to bail out the guys.

That morning the sheriff's office announced my name and address (the same as my parents') to the local paper. A day later, there it was, published on the first page. That night, my father picked up our loudly ringing home phone at 2 a.m. to hear threats directed at him, my mother, and me. "Where's your daughter? Out with the niggers? We'll take care of her and you too."

Of course, given my devotion to my friends in NAG, I certainly *was* out with my black and white friends. We were busy planning more trouble for the rule of law.

That summer, we did desegregate the bowling alley by challenging its policies, first in person and then in the courts. And we integrated many other public places in the DC area as well. Already a founding organizational member of SNCC, DC NAG had sent several of its members to the organizing meetings held in spring and summer of 1960 under the tutelage of Ella Baker. NAG continued to a separate entity, as did some of the other direct action organizations connected to SNCC, until 1963 when it became a branch of SNCC. NAG produced some of the more prominent SNCC leaders, drawing on Howard University students. They included Courtland Cox, Cleve Sellars, Mike Thelwell, and Stokely Carmichael, an especially good friend with whom I remained in touch well after the demise of SNCC in the late sixties.

Nothing ever happened to my family, but they feared for me. Over the next few years, they would reiterate their concern and try to get me to stay home, away from the more dangerous activities of the movement. I responded by accusing them of hypocrisy, saying they spoke for equality but were trying to keep me from helping create a fair world. Now I can see that they were only afraid for my safety.

Back then, I simply did not worry about injury or losing my life, and neither did many of my friends.

Were we whites in the movement more blasé about the physical consequences of our protests? I never thought about torture, something that must have been in the minds of southern blacks.

I thought: "What's the worst thing they can do to us? Kill us? That will be over in an instant, and it probably won't happen anyway. In any event, we would be heroes." How little I knew about what had happened, and would happen, to so many others.

CHAPTER 7

IT'S IN THE BAG

n October 1961, I had just entered my junior year of college when someone named Al Rosanes called the Davis Hall dormitory phone asking to talk to me. He told me that he was a member of the Boston Action Group and had heard my name in connection with the Wellesley College Civil Rights Group.

"Yes, I'm the chair," I said. "Yes, I've worked with SNCC in DC…yes, I'm interested in direct action projects."

Could he come out and talk to me?

"Well, okay."

I was a little uncertain, since adding anything in the city of Boston to my existing activities seemed like a lot. I was already visiting the South End Settlement House one afternoon a week to work with a group of young black girls. It took over an hour and some cold public transit changes to get to the city. Plus, winter was coming on, the season when I preferred to hibernate in the library. Until now, I had kept my civil rights activism focused either on Wellesley or the South.

The following Saturday afternoon, Al showed up at my dorm. We walked over to the El Café for coffee. He was a naturally speedy white guy in his mid-twenties, maybe Jewish, definitely a hipster. He had come to recruit me, and any other Wellesley students he could get, into the Boston Action Group. BAG, he said, used African American community boycotts to bring jobs to the black communities of Dorchester and Roxbury.

Despite (or perhaps because of) the cold, I felt restless and bored in the all-white environment of my elite college, so I decided to check out this opportunity to be in a relatively local, racially mixed activist group. Soon I was attending most of BAG's planning and organizing meetings in Roxbury, where I met the leaders, including Donald Shaw, a handsome man in his late twenties. There was some flirting, but nothing happened. I suspected, correctly, that he was married. Three years later, he and I were living together; in two more years we married, two years later became parents, and in another two years began the process of divorce. Back in 1961, I saw him as a charismatic, enthusiastic black activist: just my type.

That year the Boston Action Group was about to focus on two campaigns, the first against Hood Milk and the second directed at Wonder Bread. In each case, a community boycott of up to a month ultimately led to an agreement between the local Ministerial Alliance and the company to hire black employees proportional to the representation of blacks in the Boston community.

My activism had been forged in SNCC's anarchic and spontaneous "bodies-first" politic of direct action, sit-ins, and picketing. Now it incorporated the highly orchestrated, strategically planned, step-by-step and week-by-week refinements of the consumer boycott. To reduce discrimination in hiring, BAG used the economic power of the black community.

Most black people are poor or working class, then and now. Although each person lacked wealth, the combined power of the community could be leveraged for change. The brilliance of the consumer boycott derived from several features: it cost each participant little beyond choosing a different brand when buying a household staple; no participant had to worry about being beaten or arrested for making that choice; and children, adults, and old people all had multiple roles they could choose to play as consumers, purchasers and activists. A consumer boycott works best when the consumer has an easy alternative source for the boycotted item.

BAG selected the Hood Milk Company as its first target. Approximately 10% of Boston's 670,000 residents were black, but less than 1% of the 240 employees at Hood Milk were African American. Not one of the delivery drivers who brought milk to the homes and small stores in the black neighborhoods of Roxbury, Dorchester, and the South End was black. Boycotts are not easy, as the Montgomery, Alabama bus boycott of 1957 had showed: it took the black community two years of hard work and tremendous generation of resources through ride sharing and walking long miles. The boycotts of the Boston Action Group resolved more quickly, both because of their more limited aims and several local conditions that were more amenable to success.

The goal in Montgomery had been to change the seating patterns of forty years duration from segregated to open in every bus in the city. Montgomery citizens had no alternative public transit to use during their boycott, except what they imagined and then created at a community level. Our first organizing goal was simply to get Hood Milk to hire twenty black employees above the level of janitor, and as an alternative to Hood, consumers could drink Borden's Milk, already in the cooler at the corner store. Similarly, when we called for hiring changes at the Wonder Bread Bakery, customers could choose Sunbeam or Mary Jane breads, buns, and rolls rather than Wonder Bread.

My favorite role in the Hood Milk boycott, though it was

frightening, was a special research assignment. We needed to know just how many employees the company had, how many were white and how many were black. As in the bowling alley shoe rental, I put my white skin and light brown hair to use. In this action, I also drew on my student identity. This time, however, I had to lie, something I was not used to.

"Hello," I said, "my name is Nancy Stoller and I'm a student at Wellesley College. I'm writing a paper on automation. I wonder if I could visit your bottling plant and see how you bottle milk?"

"Of course, when would you like to come?"

It was as easy as that. Leaving my usual jeans and black turtleneck in my dorm room, I dressed in my knee-length plaid pleated skirt, a white Peter Pan shirt, and my favorite dark blue cardigan sweater. In my brown, leather saddlebag purse, I had a notebook and a ballpoint pen. One of the managers, John McDonough, showed me around. I dutifully took notes, but not just about pasteurization, the bottling machine, and the bottle capper. I also recorded the number of white and black employees in each section of the plant. For my efforts, I left with one of the nice paper Hood milk hats that employees wore on the assembly line. I donned that hat the following Saturday at our BAG meeting as I reported: 68 white workers in all the areas that I saw, and one black janitor. No black delivery truck drivers stocking the store coolers in the black neighborhoods of Boston, none seen bringing milk to the much larger Stop and Shop and A&P supermarkets, and none working in production.

The next step was to meet with the Ministerial Alliance, an organization that included most of the black church ministers and, significantly, all of the progressive leaders who already supported the southern freedom movement. Together the Alliance and BAG crafted demands, developed a plan for the actual boycott, and divided the tasks. The Alliance would consist of the "adults" who recruited congregants from the pulpit (and met with the companies), while the Action Group, made up largely of students would be active in the streets.

By the middle of January, we had prepared the flyers and publicity. The ministers announced the boycott in the local papers, and on the third Sunday in January they began encouraging their congregations to skip Hood and buy Borden's or other milk instead. "For how long?" congregants asked.

"Until Hood management begins to hire black as well as white."

We succeeded in getting press coverage, including interviews with both BAG leadership and the chair of the Ministerial Alliance, in *The Bay State Banner*, Boston's African American paper: a great help in reaching other segments of the community. The same week, teams of BAG members (black-black or black-white) went door to door throughout Roxbury, Dorchester, and the South End. We put flyers in mail slots, or in the crack between a front door and the doorframe. We talked to whoever was home.

It was winter, 1962. A blizzard with two and a half feet of snow had hit on January 6. The average high temperature that month was 36 degrees, and in February, it was only 34. Starting the last weekend in January and through the first half of February, I spent every Saturday with an outreach partner walking along the cold, windy, slushy streets of black neighborhoods in Roxbury or Dorchester, and climbing the stairs of older wooden triple-decker houses and worn brick apartment buildings. Those who opened their doors usually took our flyers. Some had even heard of the boycott. In the late afternoons as it got dark and even colder, we would gather for pizza in central Roxbury. Then I would get on the MTA for the hour-long ride back to Wellesley Square and my Davis Hall dormitory.

Once the boycott was launched, we continued our leafleting,

adding outreach in front of popular grocery stores in the central business areas in each of our three prime neighborhoods. Our message: No one should boycott this store, just the Hood Milk products. "Johnson's Corner Store has plenty of Borden's milk and cream."

"What about Borden's? Do they hire colored folk?" people would ask.

"Not yet, but once we take care of Hood, the biggest milk company in Boston, we'll get Borden's to fall in line too…"

By late February, sales must have dropped, because Hood Milk requested a meeting with the Ministerial Alliance and they adopted a hiring plan. Success – and in just a month! Negotiations in March and April with Borden's Dairy produced a similar agreement. Then two months later, the Ministerial Alliance and BAG turned their attention to Wonder Bread, the top provider of commercial bakery goods in the Boston area. At first, they resisted change, but a month of boycotting Wonder Bread produced another hiring agreement. Other milk companies and bakeries followed without boycotts. They had heard they were on the list of the Alliance, and soon after that, they announced their new hiring programs.

Ten years later, I discovered that a student at Harvard Business School had published an article using our Wonder Bread boycott as a case study to demonstrate that consumers who change their brand during a boycott switch basic loyalty to their new source and are unlikely to return to their old brand after the boycott ends. Conclusion: from a business point of view, it's more economical in the long run to change your hiring practices than go through a successful boycott. Although the author didn't phrase it this way, there was another message in the article as well; from an activist perspective, a successful consumer boycott has a beneficial domino effect within a consumer industry characterized by fairly similar products and multiple brands.

CHAPTER 8

THE TOOLS ARE IMAGINATION, TIME, AND ENERGY

Working with BAG brought me in touch with the Cambridge-Boston segment of the new Northern Student Movement, a group of university students who had been active in fundraising for the southern movement, sending supplies to families who were losing jobs and homes. Some branches were also participating in northern civil rights struggles. Boston NSM was the sponsor of a group of students I joined to spend the summer of 1962 in Prince Edward County, Virginia, about 150 miles west of my hometown.

Prince Edward County was one of the original counties involved in the *Brown v. Board of Education* lawsuit. On May 17th, 1954, the Supreme Court ruled unanimously in *Brown vs. Board of Education* that segregated schools were inherently unequal. That ruling explicitly included the Prince Edward County school districts. (The next day, on May 18th, was when my George Whythe Junior High teacher had talked to us about the decision.)

Back in 1954, I had no idea that Prince Edward County, in my own state of Virginia, was the site of one of the five joined lawsuits that made up this revolutionary and successful challenge to segregation. That county, nestled in a flat area just east of the Appalachian mountain range, was part of a wide swath of tobacco, cotton, and peanut plantations. While the county shared many economic and demographic characteristics with its neighbors, it was unique in its role in the national struggle for quality education for African Americans. It all began with a 1951 student strike at the county's black high school over inadequate texts and conditions. Oliver Hill of the NAACP agreed to represent the students. (In 1953-55, the Klan harassed his family by telephone and then threatened him further with a cross-burning at his home.) Together, Hill and the students filed *Dorothy E. Davis v. County School Board of Prince Edward County* in the US federal district court. Of the five consolidated lawsuits that ultimately came before the Supreme Court in *Brown, Davis* was the only one initiated by students; it was the only one to explicitly challenge segregated schools and not simply the unequal education delivered through them; and it was also the suit that took the longest to settle. It took seventeen long years of struggle before the Court's decision was finally implemented in the county in the form of officially desegregated schools, open to all students.

In 1954, schools that would be open to all throughout Virginia and the rest of the south were still years away. In 1958, four years after the *Brown v. Board of Education* decision, schools in Virginia were still segregated and school boards were trying various legal strategies to keep it that way. To reinforce its emphasis on opening schools to all, the Supreme Court ruled that year that all schools in any district must be open to all students, regardless of race. In response, several school systems, including Prince Edward County, closed all public schools in their county starting that fall.

The white students of Prince Edward began to attend free private academies held in the larger white churches (and later, in newly constructed buildings). There was no such alternative for black youth. The Reverend L. Francis Griffin, one of the adult supporters of the black students and a longtime county leader of the NAACP, joined with other community activists to form the Prince Edward County Christian Association (PECCA) to keep pushing for free open public education. By 1959, PECCA and some of the local black churches had opened "training centers" for the locked-out black students, providing basic tutoring. They didn't want a separate system of schools, but they also didn't want their children to fall completely behind in reading, writing, math, and history.

By spring of 1962, the Prince Edward County public schools had been closed for three years and the white community was busy fundraising to develop its own permanent all-white private system. Their whites-only system was never funded quite enough for all white children, and poor youth began to drop out as payment for school supplies and tuition were slowly introduced.

That same spring, the Northern Student Movement and PECCA jointly created their new summer alternative education program for black youth. They titled the schools Freedom Centers to make it clear they were not full-fledged schools, and that folks were still fighting for real public schools funded by county tax dollars. The local civil rights activists' long-term desegregation goal was a fully funded integrated public school system for all children, black and white, rich and poor.

The summer program was a stopgap project designed to give a lift to the community struggle by bringing in extra resources, developing some publicity, and building more national support for the ongoing legal campaign. Although most of the national attention in the civil rights movement in 1962 was on Freedom Riders (several of whom came from DC NAG) and organizing in Alabama and Mississippi, the black citizens of Prince Edward County had their own rows to hoe, a little off to the side, out of the national media spotlight.

Created in 1961, the Northern Student Movement primarily mobilized northern students to support the civil rights struggle. Boston NSM first sent books to southern civil rights organizations. When they learned about the ongoing school closure in Prince Edward County, NSM leaders helped sponsor a speaking tour in the north for Rev. Griffin and decided to offer specific assistance to the community. Griffin responded: Could they send him some college students for a summer teaching project? Yes, they said. And so the 1962 project of Summer Freedom Centers in Prince Edward County was born. In a typical SNCC-style organizing model, the local organization – in this case, PECCA – was the ultimate decision-maker. The out-of-town organization provided agreed-upon assistance: money, supplies, and labor in the form of student volunteers.

I applied to the national office of the NSM in February 1962 to go to Prince Edward County for the summer. In addition to my general civil rights organizing, I emphasized my past sit-in experience, my Virginia background, and my demonstrated ability to work in an interracial organization in both the North and the Upper South. On the other hand, I had to admit that I had no teaching experience at all. To my great excitement, I got selected to be a member of the group. Most of the participants were already in graduate or professional school, with several Harvard Law students and three participants from the Harvard School of Education. There were twelve of us, all from the Boston area.

As well-educated volunteers from prestigious New England colleges and law schools, we were told that we could expect to teach classes. We were assigned groups of children according to our skills and their needs. A senior teacher would supervise us. Each volunteer ultimately inhabited a collection of roles: apprentice, teacher, witness, visiting cultural outsider, and inevitably, target of white hostility toward Yankees. Fortunately for our survival, the locals had no qualms about protecting us or telling us how to act. For example, no mixed gender-race groups in the same car. And no mixed hanging out on the front porch, even within one gender.

Organizers told me not to worry about my teaching skills, the project would take care of that, and amazingly, it did. Educated and "re-educated" at the Highlander Folk Center near Knoxville, Tennessee, we learned to teach without regular texts or books. (Seven years before Paolo Friere's *Pedagogy of the Oppressed* appeared in English, we were being schooled in *conscientization* and how to teach literacy from the newspaper or family conversations.) In addition, the Highlander staff schooled us in its traditions of diversity and social justice work, and taught us some of the broader history of the labor movement in the South and its connections with anti-segregation work since the 1930s. I had always thought about my activism through a lens of black and white student rebellion against Jim Crow, segregation, prejudice, and slow-moving adults. Now I discovered that what we were doing had a long history, and that many older folks had been, and were still, quite involved in this work. I realized that the history of the poor and black in my own region was a blank space in my mind, except for my rudimentary understanding of the founding of the colonies, the Revolutionary War, the state history of Virginia, and the Civil War (all from a white and southern perspective, of course).

We spent only a week at Highlander, but I left a much different person than the Nancy Stoller who had arrived. I now had some idea of how to teach reading and writing without texts. I had a sense that I was being supported in some way by people who knew what they were doing and wouldn't let me fail. In addition, I now thought of myself as a participant in a larger, multi-generational world. I still had my civil rights life and worldview, in contrast to the white world and its values. Now I sensed that I was also part of a social justice movement throughout the South, in little towns and rural areas, on plantations and in the piney woods, as well as in cities and in both black and white communities. That social justice movement almost felt a little too big. I didn't want to lose my black-white focus within it, but I was being told I wouldn't have to. I was learning that there was also a long history of black and white working together, in addition to the official history of "necessary" white societal management that I knew so well. At Highlander, I was discovering the earlier generations of people I needed to know – and know about – in order to become who I wanted to be.

CHAPTER 9

TEACHING AT CROSSROADS BAPTIST CHURCH

When we arrived in Prince Edward County, I found my room in a small boarding house in Farmville, the county seat. An older white woman, who was trying to make do after the recent death of her husband, ran the house. Within a week, she was forced to evict me and the other white female volunteer. I moved to the finished basement in a black family home and my roommate went to another residence. My hosts, the Gowans, seemed surprised to see me, but they were still very friendly. The words "brave" and "gracious" best describe them. They had stepped up when asked by their minister, the ever-persuasive Rev. Griffin, and they looked after me every day, providing a foldaway bed and my breakfasts and dinners throughout the summer.

The leaders of the summer project assigned me to a class of six to nine-year-olds. (The five-year-olds had their own kindergarten class.) I had fifteen students. None had ever been to a nursery school, kindergarten, or regular school.

Crossroads Baptist Church, a whitewashed wood frame building, had a sanctuary for about fifty people. Shaded by several oak trees, it sat at the intersection of two roads, one gravel and one dirt, both of which passed through large tobacco plantations. The church housed a total of three classes, each with fifteen to twenty students. Two groups met in small classrooms like mine, and the third group, comprised of young teenagers, met in the sanctuary. Another Freedom Center, with five or six classes, was located at a slightly larger church in another part of the county.

✦

The Freedom Centers project had arranged some donated supplies: crayons, paper, pencils, chalk, a few blackboards, large newsprint tablets, paint, and some new books. Local teachers brought over the old school books they had saved from the closed black schools. They had been using them for tutoring over the previous three years.

For my class, I had ten new Easy Reader picture books. Many of my students came from sharecropper families who could not afford to buy any books at all. The children were thrilled to see these brand new picture books. A child might sit on the floor (we only had a few chairs), open a book on her lap, and drift away from everything else in the room, into the picture inside. For many of my students, this was how they began their day at the Crossroads Church Freedom Center, just looking at a book.

The first day, I took my students on a little walk past the parking lot (we never went out of sight of the church), where we picked up leaves. We came back to our room, where they traced or drew and colored their leaves, while I wrote the word "leaf" on the newsprint paper on the wall. "Can you copy this word?" I asked. I watched as some students just kept drawing and coloring, and a few tried to copy the word "leaf." This was not the best assignment to start with. Several seemed disappointed in themselves, even though I complimented everyone on whatever was on the page. After that, I would ask the student the title or description of his or her artwork, and then either write it out for the child to copy or write it on the drawing, whatever and wherever the student wished.

One of our goals was to teach every child to write his or her name during the eight-week program. Gradually, I figured out what each student knew or didn't know. Only three of my students could read. I sorted out the ones who could recognize letters or numbers and those who could not. Bit by bit, everyone learned how to make a personal signature of some sort and began proudly signing their papers and drawings. Students who could read helped those who could not. Those who knew numbers taught those who didn't.

One day, for our math lesson, we collected and counted pebbles. Another day, we discussed teeth. I had asked students to talk about what they did before coming to school that morning. "Did you brush your teeth?" I asked. In a matter of minutes, I felt my privilege in an embarrassing way. Only one of my students had his own toothbrush. A few others shared. The rest lived in households with no toothbrushes.

Most students, even the littlest ones, walked to school, and the walk was up to a mile. What was most striking to me was the incredible enthusiasm of all the students, from the five-year-olds to the teenagers. Having been shut out of school for so long, they were eager to learn, either with us or in a regular school. They knew how valuable these skills were. Their parents and older siblings had been fighting for better schools and civil rights for years. Even the youngest children knew that there was a US government located somewhere far away that was on their side. They seemed to have confidence that they would eventually win.

In my years as a professor, organizer, and activist, I have drawn repeatedly on the teaching philosophy I learned at Highlander and on the practice I gained in Prince Edward County. Most importantly, teaching in Prince Edward County that summer schooled me in a kind of learning democracy that gives the same respect to an illiterate six-year-old's curiosities, skills, and ideas as to those of a twenty-year-old from an elite white college. I've tried to bring my faith in this kind of democratic learning and teaching with me into every group and organization to which I've belonged.

CHAPTER 10

THE VOTER REGISTRATION SURVEY: A CASE OF "MAKING IT UP"

Another addition to my skills that summer was the discovery that I could do valuable research. This was twenty years before I heard the term "action research" and five years before I had the nerve to say in graduate school that no one needs a degree to design a research project or conduct a valuable survey. Two years before, I had taken my first research methods class. The local people who gave me my assignment knew I could do it well before I did, and they also knew just what they wanted. The civil rights movement always seemed to be putting people in situations where something new just had to be done. When asked at the fiftieth anniversary of its founding how SNCC workers figured out various techniques, Cortland Cox provided the best – and to me, the most accurate – answer: "We just made it up."

About halfway through the summer, a PECCA member approached me. They were going to start a voter registration drive, and wanted to get a sense of how many people might register. Would I design a survey for them?

"Me? Why me?" I asked.

"Well, someone said that you studied sociology in college. So you know how to design a survey, right?"

In my mind, the task was way beyond my ability. Yes, I had just taken a statistics course, and I had read the results of some surveys, but creating and analyzing a survey seemed to be what a professional did – an academic, a teacher, a trained sociologist, or psychologist, someone far above me in knowledge and skill. Well, I was told, you know more about this than anyone else here, as far as we know. If anyone can do it right, it's you.

"Okay," I said. I would have been ashamed not to try.

Within a week, I had made a simple survey form that we mimeographed for distribution to teams of interviewers. There was space to record an address, names, ages, number of adults in the house, and whether anyone had registered to vote or was interested in registering. The next week teams began to go out, always two people. At least one would be a local person, and if available, one of our northern volunteers would fill in as the second. The majority of visitors went to plantations at the homes of sharecroppers. People were invariably polite, but often suspicious and uncertain, at least when I was part of the team. I remember that the all-local teams had the best results in eliciting interest in registration.

My other job in the survey project was to collect and count up the results. I don't remember what they were; I do remember that PECCA was happy that the survey had been done. They used it to map their recruitment plan for the voter registration campaign, which got into full swing that fall.

For me, this survey project, from beginning to end, set the style for my future research career. Initiated by a community group; designed with community benefit in mind; overseen, revised, and implemented with the community organization;

using input from those with technical skills to get a quality product; and put to use for a practical purpose. In addition, it didn't have to – and could not – be perfect. It was better to act than do nothing.

That summer, I learned several major lessons about where I fit in the world. I was part of a bigger movement than I had known. I could teach – and what I learned about teaching could be applied in other settings, too. I could do research that people might want. And I could work and live in a black rural town as long as I had the support of the local community.

When I think of all the things I learned that summer, I'm reminded in a deeply personal way of what Cortland said at the fiftieth anniversary of the founding of SNCC: "We just made it up. The tools are imagination, time and energy." Cortland was speaking of how SNCC organized, but I think his words were true for the movement as a whole, too. Each person was called on, or called upon herself, to try new things, to move beyond what she thought she could do. And by moving beyond, we each created something completely new in ourselves and around us. This was, and is, the deepest lesson for me from the early sixties.

Nancy's parents, Ruth Klarberg and Morton
Stoller, wedding photo, November, 1938

Nancy's father Mort flying radio-controlled
airplane, Hampton VA, 1938

Twin brothers Bob and Pete with Mom on
front steps, Stuart Gardens, 1941

37 Alleghany Rd., Hampton, VA, with Nancy and mother Ruth, 1943

Nancy with brothers Pete and Bob in back yard

Grandparents Stoller garden, Bob, Nancy, Pete,
Richmond Hill, Queens, NY, 1946

Freedom Center School, Farmville VA, 1962

SNCC I.D. photo: "Just in case you don't come
back" photo, Little Rock AK, 1964

Nancy and Kwame's wedding, 1966

Nancy and newborn daughter Gwendolyn, 1968

Nancy and Gwendolyn, Tangier, Morocco, 1969

CHAPTER 11

AFTER MORT

B y September, I was back at Wellesley, entering my senior
year. I thought it would be all about writing my honors thesis on the difference between moral and legal guilt, a topic I
had chosen because of my interest in the rationalizations of
participants in two "legal" systems that I thought abhorrent: the
killing machine of the Holocaust, and the legal infrastructure
of the racist American South. I also imagined another year as a
nurse's aide, applying to graduate school, maybe in philosophy
but more likely in sociology. I would pursue my light romance
with a black Harvard Law student I had met in Prince Edward
County and continue my local and Southern activism. In early
October, however, doctors informed my parents that the swell-
ing under my father's chin was a melanoma tumor in his lymph
gland. It was the result of a missed diagnosis ten years before.
The cancer was metastatic. Although I didn't realize it then, he
only had ten months to live.

My father embarked on a series of treatments that might
keep him alive. There was surgery and chemo. The worst for
me was to see one of the horrific insulin shock treatments that

reduced him to a limp unconscious body on a cot. That treatment was sometimes used to complement the electroshock at the Wiswall Mental Hospital, where I worked as a nurses' aide. I instinctively knew that its experimental use on my father was a sign of desperation, and that there was no real chance he would survive. Why couldn't they just leave him alone? And why couldn't he just get better somehow?

When my great-aunt Pauline came from New York to Maryland to see him in the final months, it was my job to host her. She raged with anger that he had been misdiagnosed. (Because the pathology report had been misread, the surgeon had not cleared the edges of the original mole. All the information was still in his medical records, so there was no doubt.) He was only 46 years old.

That last year at Wellesley remains the saddest in my life. My father was dying and in treatment all year. Both parents insisted I stay in school. I managed to pass my classes and apply to graduate school, but I dropped out of everything else, including all my political activity. With great effort, I did manage to finish my honors thesis on legal and moral guilt. Although my advisor admired the final product and my department accepted it, the interdepartmental college committee rejected it, stating it was too short –only 55 pages – and needed more footnotes. I was humiliated on my day of graduation when my name didn't appear in the program, where it would have if I had gained the final committee approval. No one but my advisor objected. None of my friends noticed. I had managed to tell my advisor about my father, and had cried in her office when she told me about the committee's rejection. I simply couldn't talk about my sense of failure with my friends. Telling them my father was ill was about all I could manage.

My mother had flown up to see me graduate, which I later realized to be an incredibly difficult task for her emotionally.

While I wanted her to be proud of me, I realize that she was barely holding herself together for the afternoon event. Graduation was a blur of sadness. All my successes, Phi Beta Kappa, highest honors, graduate school admission, seemed to mean nothing. As I waited on the library steps to hear my name and receive my scroll, I could see my mother's erect body turned toward me in a folding chair beneath the shade of the rhododendron dell. She was unmoving, talking to no one, just looking ahead. She had flown in to Boston to see me graduate, then left the same afternoon. My father's impending death, which happened only a week later, had been kept from me, so I only half understood why she insisted on returning to the airport so quickly.

While my friends were celebrating with extended family, dinners, and parties, I cried, walked back alone to my dorm room, and stared at my suitcase and boxes. I was acutely lonely. I packed up my books, awards, papers, and clothes and took the bus home the next day. Eight more lonely hours on the Greyhound. Perhaps someone met me at the station. I have no memory of that, but I know my life and emotional state was of little interest to anyone else. We were each riding a slowed-up carousel of pain and loss outside and inside Room 2014 at the National Institutes of Health Medical Center.

My father was already in the hospital for his last stay when I arrived. My brother Bob had been living at home most of the year, and Pete arrived from somewhere recently, perhaps even before me. Every day involved a trip and vigil at the hospital. The cancer had left Mort paralyzed on his left side. His thin face, scarred neck, and limp hand confused me. I couldn't look away. Two years later, in therapy after a series of migraines, a psychoanalyst suggested that my neurological symptoms of tingling and numbness on my right cheek and hand might be mirror images of my father from those days.

My mother seemed more desperate every day, sitting, wandering the hospital halls. I know now she was trying to get the doctors to approve some treatment to help my father die because he was in so much pain. This was the beginning of her journey to the membership and activism in the Hemlock Society.

A day or two before his death, Mort gave instructions to us children: be sure to mow the lawn; the house needs to be painted next year. It was only then I realized he really was about to die. At the actual moment of his death, I was home taking a nap, after an all-night stay at the hospital. Guilt intensified and warped my grief further. Years later, I also missed my mother's moment of death by walking back too slowly from lunch. I know rationally that these absences weren't my fault, but even now, 52 years after my father's death and ten years after my mother's, I still feel guilty.

From the NASA history page:

Morton J. Stoller (1917-1963) was a leading figure in the Nation's weather and communications satellite program. He joined the National Advisory Committee for Aeronautics in 1939, as an electrical engineer, at the Langley Aeronautical Laboratory, and in 1958 became NASA's chief of space science in the office of the assistant director for Space Science. In early 1960 he was named assistant director for the satellite and Sounding Rocket program, in the Office of Space Flight, and in 1962 was named director of the Office of Applications.

After my father's memorial, I was desperate to join my SNCC friends on the second series of Freedom Rides. May Goldberg, who had known my parents since before I was born, informed me, "Absolutely not! You have to stay here with your mother. She needs you." I understood the logic, but I hated it. It would be a long summer in Washington, DC.

During those ten months of my father's illness, Fred Wallace, my African American boyfriend who I'd met in Prince Edward County, had been reassessing our relationship. He made it clear that when he moved on from Harvard Law School to a New York City job after graduation, our romance would be over. He knew he would never marry a white woman. He wanted to be a leader in the black community wherever he lived, and he was sure that an interracial relationship would never work. I remember being shocked on ethical grounds. How could someone just make a rational decision like that, especially when we had been working together against racism and for equality? It was completely clear that he meant it. It wasn't just that he didn't "love" me: he had no interest in loving me or in being with me. I could be a friend of some sort. Maybe.

Two years later I visited Fred in New York and learned he had joined the Republican Party. He didn't care about their values. In Fred's mind, all white organizations were equally useless and usable. The Republicans were a group through which a black lawyer could move ahead more easily than he could in the Democratic Party: less competition from other blacks. Years later, I tried to track him down, both in New York and in his home state of Ohio, but he had disappeared into another life. I guess he didn't become a famous politician. One thing was certain; in the summer of 1963, he wasn't the slightest bit interested in providing me with any care or sympathy for the loss of my father. I stopped communicating with him completely.

So in the summer of 1963, I lost both my father and my fantasy of marrying Fred, or of even being loved by him. In fact, I seemed to have no one to lean on. My brothers were far away. My mother was more in need of a shoulder than able to provide one. Instead of escaping Ruth's depression and my own grief by going South, where I could get beat up on a bus and ignore my internal pain, I spent the summer as a paid intern at a non-profit soft-money K Street research firm, the Bureau of Social Science Research. I continued to stay active with SNCC projects on evenings and weekends, sitting in at restaurants as part of the Maryland Route 44 movement, sending supplies south, and helping desegregate an apartment complex. I did not discuss these ventures at work, where one was supposed to be "neutral" about politics. I had my DC-area friends who I'd met back at Glen Echo. We managed to take a camping trip to the mountains once, where I was reminded of the experience of joy in nature together with a group who I could be completely at home with.

The Bureau of Social Science Research provided my first experience of the professional research world. My main job was to be an assistant to a project director, Sam Klausner, who had a significant grant from the Defense Department studying how people react to stress. The three branches of the study included skydivers, men training to invade Cuba, and a third branch that I don't remember. I never got clearance to go to Florida to study the invasion group, but I did go up in a small plane to watch my boss jump out and float down with a parachute as a way of convincing skydivers that he could be trusted.

In early August, I convinced my colleagues at the BSSR that we should study the March on Washington, the first big civil rights march and the one where Martin Luther King gave his "I Have A Dream" speech. I was really keen on this event because it was partly organized by SNCC and other direct action groups from throughout the South, including King's group, the Southern Christian Leadership Conference, as well as by traditional African American advocacy organizations such as the NAACP, the Urban League, CORE, and A. Philip Randolph of the Sleeping Car Porters. I knew it would be big.

At the BSSR, we made a variety of data collection tools,

including observation cards to assess the numbers, density, and demographic composition of the attendees. I organized a process to collect press coverage as well. Someone else took photos. I was able to recruit about ten people from the Bureau for the day of the march. Everything went smoothly, both at the huge demonstration and with our research plan. We returned with several boxes of raw data.

Soon after, my job ended and I went off to graduate school. The research we had done at the March? It sat in those boxes. The following year when I asked if I could analyze it and write an academic paper about what we had seen and learned, the director of the Bureau curtly informed me that those materials belonged to them and that they had no intention of letting me use them. To this day, in 2017, I know of no publications based on that mound of data about that nationally important march, because its official "owners" weren't interested. This was another important lesson about research and activism. It was the opposite of what I had learned in Farmville, where the goal was to always do something with what you collected, and narrow terms of ownership were considered selfish at best. I vowed I would never again organize a research project without knowing what would, or could, be done with the data. Starting the day that the Bureau said no, a part of me knew that I would generally have higher hopes for the usefulness of research that originated from minority communities.

1962-63 had brought some painful losses: my father's illness and death, my naiveté about interracial relationships, and a loss of confidence in my capacity for independent scholarship when my thesis was rejected. The following year brought the frustrating, but less painful, end of my belief that the social organization of research and science was open and democratic, thanks to the actions of the Social Science Research Bureau.

In fall 1963, I was about to begin a new phase of my life,

graduate school in sociology, where I hoped I would learn some approaches that would help me think, write, and find employment in this strange world I seemed to be in.

CHAPTER 12

HOW I BECAME A CERTIFIED
ACTIVIST INTELLECTUAL

n the fall of 1963, I moved my academic home from the town of Wellesley to nearby Waltham, Mass. and the Brandeis University Sociology Department, where my professional identity emerged as a civil rights activist, researcher, and teacher. I found a Cambridge apartment for the year with a friend from the DC movement, Mary Heller, and another friend from Wellesley, Angie King. I felt lonely. I was still in shock over the loss of my father.

I knew none of the students in my graduate program or cohort. Besides knowing my roommates, I was connected to other activists in BAG. They didn't seem especially interested in my family losses, but Donald Shaw kept calling. During the year, I saw him more and more. We gradually became a couple. He had separated from his wife; soon, he began the divorce process. Much later, I realized there was more overlap than I thought. Back then, I was enamored, and I really wanted to spend time each week with someone who cared about me.

Fortunately for my sense of self-worth, I was becoming more and more involved in my life as an aspiring sociologist. Unlike most of my teachers at Wellesley and my employers at the BSSR, this group actually seemed to respect my intelligence, take an interest in me personally, and want to develop my skills. Each was passing on what he knew (all my professors were men). They encouraged hard work and rewarded it with appreciation for my technical development, thinking, and values, and for my growing ability to move from theory to research to practice and back again. I was happy.

I sometimes wonder what would have happened had I gone to my other option for graduate school: Columbia University. There, the emphasis was on Sociology as Science. Quantification was king. At Brandeis, there were two major foci: social theory, led by a group of Jewish intellectual refugees from Germany, and field work, supervised by a less traumatically displaced group of sociologists primarily from the University of Chicago. The first group included Lewis Coser, Kurt Wolff, Egon Bittner, and later, Herbert Marcuse. The second group was led by Everett Hughes, Murray Schwartz, and Maurice Stein. Phil Slater and Gordon Fellman occupied the edges of both groups. Others, including Rosabeth Kantor, passed through briefly on the way to other careers. My graduate student cohort and those just before and after, only the third sociology cohort at the University, included major feminist scholars-to-be such as Barrie Thorne and Nancy Chodorow. My professors championed the civil rights movement even when they made intense critiques of us graduate students who wrote about it. I couldn't have found a better place to integrate the disparate parts of myself.

I was interested in the field study emphasis within the research methodology options. For most of my graduate training, I was supported by a fellowship from the National Institutes of Mental Health that focused on training sociology graduate students in a field methodology that was somewhat similar to that used by anthropologists, but applied in urban settings and the study of large-scale institutions. I used this approach for almost every research project I pursued throughout my career. During the second half of my first year in the department, I helped form a new student entity: The Crisis Research Group. Using the notion of the participant observation continuum, in which we had been drilled during our first semester, we decided to select demonstrations for study and then planned roles for ourselves that ranged from 100% participation to 100% observation. (Naturally, I always wanted to be as close to a 100% participant as possible.) Then we would attend, observe, write notes, and generate a multi-perspectival report. Because it was the mid-sixties, we had plenty of demonstrations to choose from. We began practicing with some Boston-area events, and the plan seemed to work pretty well. We agreed that we could keep our group together in the fall, and I reluctantly returned to Maryland to keep my mother company, forced to miss the experience of 1964 Mississippi Freedom Summer and eager to return to the field.

Soon after I returned to Massachusetts for my second year of graduate school, I heard about a major demonstration in New York. I thought it was perfect for our Crisis Research Group. I convinced fourteen students to join me for a Crisis Research Group weekend. We would study the first day of the 1964 World's Fair in New York, where the Bronx and Brooklyn chapters of the Congress of Racial Equality had organized a stall-in to protest inadequate hiring of blacks in the building of the fair infrastructure. Our professors agreed that this research venture was a good use of our time. I was ecstatic. We spent a few weeks preparing. Indeed, in many ways we were probably better organized than the CORE chapters that officially sponsored the stall-in. They were in conflict with each other and with other civil rights groups about whether the stall-in was a good idea at all. "Would it create bad traffic and be a public relations flop?" "Why should we harm visitors to the Fair?" "There were more jobs now and the management of the fair has improved." We students knew that as long as the stall-in was going to happen in any form, the Crisis Research Group would be there, and we could learn something worthwhile.

On October 1, the first day of the Fair, I intentionally stalled out my red 1960 Volkswagen Bug in the middle east-bound lane of the brand new Brooklyn-Queens Expressway in order to block the highway. My passenger was Marty Nicolaus, another sociology graduate student (who went on to ultra-leftwing politics and translated Marx's *Grundrisse*). Other graduate student members of our team helped stop a subway, observed on overpasses, collected newspapers, watched television coverage, and took notes and photos from inside the fair. Later, I wrote a research paper about the first day of the Fair, showing how differently it appeared from fourteen different vantage points. The stall-in itself was a mixed success. The overall disruption was huge. But attendance was much lower than had been projected before announcement of the demonstration. Our research team comprised about a quarter of the total participants. Due to tremendous publicity about the stall-in, many potential first-day attendees stayed home, which meant my highway tactic had little effect.

Graduate school and my side activities were teaching me a lot, but I was desperately restless, and I continued to mourn my father. Over a year after his death, I was still talking to him in the stars, that enormous space where I still think his electrons are floating in the 21st century. Don Shaw and I were now a recognized couple with an open-ended future. But I didn't feel very happy about that future. Something was nagging me. I had a series of low-grade migraine headaches. I wanted to get away from the North, from academia, from Don, and from my roommates. I wanted to go back to the South, where everything I really loved was happening.

Two months after the World's Fair opened, I dropped out of graduate school for the rest of the year and went to work full-time for SNCC. I spoke with Stokely Carmichael about my interest in working for SNCC for a while. Soon he arranged for me to join the paid staff in Arkansas, at a salary of $10/week plus housing and beginning in December. Instead of attending classes and writing field notes and term papers for my professors, I would be writing memos, delivering supplies, sitting-in, and sending letters home. I was sure this move south would give me a much-needed break from the malaise of my daily life.

CHAPTER 13

ARKANSAS TRAVELER

By 1964, SNCC had grown enormously from its origins in early 1960, evolving from a loose collection of direct action organizations to a central office in Atlanta with paid field workers coordinating large projects throughout the South. Although the Mississippi Freedom Summer brought massive attention and funds to the organization, it also strained SNCC's internal management skills and leadership, especially as some volunteers refused to go home after the summer, insisting that no one could tell them what to do. SNCC leaders were faced with "too many" (white) hangover volunteers from the Freedom Summer project. Even though I was white, I gained a staff position because I had a long history with the organization and a reputation as a responsible organizer. Most importantly, Stokely Carmichael, a core member of SNCC's leadership team and soon to be the organization's chair, had vouched for me.

I attended SNCC's December 1964 conference in Waveland, Mississippi the first week after I began my new affiliation with the Arkansas project. Intense emotions characterized this all-SNCC conference, as did heavy drinking every night. There were daily – and nightly – discussions about internal democracy and education or privilege as unacknowledged but powerful sources of power within the organization; white-black dynamics; grassroots leadership challenges; the difficulties of rapid growth; and the relationship between the Atlanta office and the field projects. Several projects had recently experienced violent attacks. The memory of the deaths of Chaney, Goodman, and Schwerner remained fresh; their bodies had been found in August, just four months before, and no progress had been made toward any arrests. Regular SNCC staff had managed over 400 northern volunteers for three months and were feeling the psychological and emotional consequences. Some people seemed to be at a breaking point emotionally.

Arkansas was in the hinterlands of SNCC publicity and consciousness, and in some ways, this might have been a good thing for the members of the project there. I'd heard that the project itself was much calmer than others. On the other hand, the state was not thought of as the Deep South, even though its eastern half was dominated by the Mississippi Delta and the inevitable dangers created by plantation economies, voting restrictions, and severe poverty. Once again, I was on my way to a project and a state that were marginalized in both the national consciousness and in SNCC. My past SNCC work had been in the upper south of Virginia and Maryland, where segregation and violence were real, but less known and less brutal than the deeper South. I didn't select these sites myself, but I sometimes wonder how my life would have turned out if I had worked in the deep South, where volunteers were known as freedom fighters. Would my psychology be different? Certainly my movement network and reputation would be different.

By January 1, I began my duties in Arkansas, all of which occurred either in Little Rock, where SNCC had its main office, or in the Delta cities of Pine Bluff, West Helena, and Forrest

City. The first day, I got my photo taken, "just in case you disappear and we need to use it."

I began to collect my salary: $10/week. I moved into a one-bedroom shared SNCC apartment in an all-black housing complex across the street from Philander Smith College, also mostly black. My roommate was Arlene Wilgoren, another white woman, from Boston. We often had others sleeping on the living room floor. Our favorite meal was macaroni, spaghetti sauce, and ground beef. It could be stretched forever with more macaroni and sauce. Next door, someone played "My Girl" by the Temptations every morning at 7: my wake-up call. Our neighbors also taught us to play bid whist, and we had frequent Saturday games.

Other members of the project during that time included Bill and Ruthie Hansen, Jim Jones, and Ben Grinage. During the last three months of my time in Arkansas, my boyfriend Don participated, too. He had missed me, and he wanted to be part of the southern movement. He was assigned to the West Helena and Forrest City offices of SNCC partly because we were all afraid that if he and I were in the same city, we might forget to stay far apart, and the consequences could be dangerous – especially for him, but for the rest of our project as well. I had a mixed reaction to his arrival in the state. I had left Boston partly to get away from him, and now here he was. My inability to confront my mixed feelings made me unable to do anything about it.

My primary job, assigned to me by the SNCC office in Atlanta, was coordinating the Freedom Centers within the state. This meant getting supplies distributed and dealing with our entire infrastructure: phones, furniture, transportation, and various other communication challenges. The United Auto Workers (UAW) in Detroit donated four dark green Dodge V8 sedans to our project, chosen because they were the fastest cars of their type. We had a lot of driving to do around the state, and we wanted to be able to outrun the KKK or, if necessary, the police. Several times I rode in cars that were being followed, experiencing the 100 mph speeds of these Dodges, which were being sold in the North to local police departments. They also sent us a bright yellow 3/4-ton truck so we could deliver supplies. Because of my job, I got first rights on driving the truck, which was a big thrill. Its engine was so powerful I had to start it in second gear to avoid sudden leaps forward.

One of the great things about SNCC was that when a person could do something, SNCC philosophy made it clear that no one could say, well, he isn't educated, or she's just a woman. Women in SNCC asserted their skills and got respect. Most of the people I worked with were just too busy trying to get things done to consciously hold on to traditional roles. In fact, from the start, it was a set of traditional roles – of racial subservience – that SNCC challenged. As the required racial roles lost value in the civil rights movement, people seemed to feel that expecting subservience by young people and women was also inappropriate. In fact, it was often youth of both sexes who led in organizing. An examination of photos from voter registration lines in the rural south shows that more than half of those in line were older women. I felt I often got more respect from African American coworkers, male and female, than from white men in our project. I think that there was a deeper respect in the black community for the strengths of women, black or white, than there was in the white world. SNCC was at the center of a broad movement for radical democracy, which affected its internal politics as well as its external actions.

The Freedom Centers provided political education, organizing, voter registration, and programs for children. They also held meetings to plan direct action, including some sit-ins. The central office put out *The Arkansas Voice*, a monthly newspaper modeled on *The Student Voice*, which was published at SNCC's Atlanta office. We started our state paper primarily because someone donated a press. Atlanta then sent us a volunteer who helped us figure out how to make it work; the next thing I knew, I was writing articles on our various projects around the state, doing mockups, and running the press itself.

In late February, we learned that the cafeteria in the State Capitol remained segregated. No blacks allowed. Given that the Public Accommodations Act (part of the Civil Rights Act of 1964) had been passed a year earlier, that the sit-in movement was five years old, and this was, after all, the *state capitol,* we knew we had to do something. We discovered that the local NAACP had filed a suit over a year before, but it had languished in the back rooms of the courthouse. We decided to publicize the situation. We developed a plan and discussed our options. What if we were arrested? What if we were just served? What if we just had to stand there all day? Then we selected a day to have our sit-in.

On March 11, 1965, a group of about fifteen SNCC workers and Little Rock supporters arrived at the cafeteria at 11:30, just before the lunch rush. First we confirmed the segregationist policy: I selected an item and paid for it. I carefully pocketed my receipt. Then a black member of our group entered the line and selected an item. The cashier refused to serve him. We both stepped out into the hallway. Then the rest of our mixed group joined the two of us at the start of the cafeteria line. The line came to a complete halt. After a while someone closed the door, leaving us just outside the cafeteria, standing patiently in the basement of the Capitol. Now no one was being served, black or white. I don't remember how long we stood there, but I remember well that suddenly the hallway behind us filled with state troopers telling us to "Leave now!" No one moved. We were sure we'd be arrested. Instead, they started hitting us with billy clubs and driving us up the stairs. Eventually we found ourselves outside the now-blocked doors of the capitol on its broad patio and wide steps leading down to the street. Beaten up and thrown out! This was an option we hadn't imagined.

We walked back to the SNCC office to make a new plan. For the next two days we went again to the cafeteria just before lunch, each time recruiting new people willing to be beaten by the police. The third time, an unknown person released some sort of gas fumes into the inside stairs. The air filled with droplets that stung the eyes and made breathing difficult. It wasn't tear gas, but something worse. Soon we were not only hit and bruised, but also gasping and vomiting.

To our ultimate advantage, the gas affected the troopers as well as us. Orval Faubus, the famous segregationist governor of Arkansas who had been sending in the troopers every day, decided to shut the doors of the cafeteria to all for the moment, because "some people had been hurt." ("Some people" meant the state police.) With the help of this attacker, we had succeeded in making it clear that the cafeteria could not operate as usual if it remained segregated.

Within a few weeks, the long stalled public accommodations case came before a judge in Little Rock. As a white person, I testified about being able to buy lunch, while the black SNCC worker gave his testimony about being denied service immediately behind me in line. The judge even examined my receipt for a cup of coffee. Within a few days, the decision came back: The cafeteria must be open to all or stay closed. The following Monday it re-opened, now for everyone, never to return to its segregated ways. The opening was completely peaceful. This victory showed us all how activism can push policy and litigation ahead.

While most of my memories of life in SNCC during my four years of active involvement in the movement center on the bravery, creativity, and hard work of staff, volunteers, and local community members, there was also a painful side. There were many internal conflicts – arguments about priorities, race, sexism, and whether to tolerate the whims and personalities of various volunteers and staff. There was also competition for publicity and leadership.

At Waveland, for example, aside from the lengthy processing and arguments about the shape of SNCC membership and leadership, many people got drunk. A fire started in one of the rooms; I remember seeing the ashes. At least one woman reported being raped. We all knew that these incidents resulted from the enormous stress that the staff had been under during the preceding summer and into the fall. No matter how difficult things were within the organization, we always had to figure out how to solve our problems internally because we couldn't afford negative publicity. Even violence within the organization had to be kept hidden. I had to face this personally as a victim of violence from a local volunteer while I was working in Arkansas.

One night in Little Rock, someone organized a party. It was mostly students from Philander Smith College. SNCC workers who lived in the apartments across the street were also invited. I remember going with my roommate, Arlene. Don was still in Boston. Someone, a guy from the college who had been to some of our actions and occasionally hung out at our main office, walked me back to my apartment. (I'll call him Y.) As I stepped inside the door to the empty living room, Y leaned in and kissed me. I wasn't interested and quickly stepped back. He stepped in and pulled the door shut behind him. I tried to say good night and open the door to get him out, but Y guarded it with his back and started pushing me toward the apartment's bedroom. I struggled and told him to leave. This struggle went on for what seemed like ten to fifteen minutes and included my running to our living room balcony and calling out the window for help. No one responded.

I remember being shocked right then that, although there were lights on around the apartment complex, no one came to a window or called out "Are you okay?"

Everyone in the complex knew which was the SNCC apartment, and that two white women lived there. We were the only whites in the entire apartment complex at that time. (Later we also had a white male roommate.) I felt a sinking sensation: no one wanted to get involved. No one cared that I was calling for help. Or maybe they cared but didn't have the courage, or the foolishness, to act.

Eventually, Y did rape me on one of our mattresses. Then he got up, said goodbye as if it were all something normal, and left. It was if my "No's" were just a usual part of the process. I felt so defeated. Not only did he seem to feel imperviously casual about this, but I knew that my options to respond were severely limited.

I couldn't call the police, after all. He was black and I was white. It would be a disaster all around: for him as a black man accused of assaulting a white woman; for me as a white female member of a civil rights organization and therefore considered a "nigger lover"; and for our local SNCC project and the Little Rock black community, because it would take attention away from the movement and put it on this sordid mess. I talked with my roommate, who listened sympathetically. By the next day, I knew what I wanted, and I got it.

I requested that SNCC ban Y from the office and from any activity that SNCC was involved with. He would not be able to come to any rally, march, demonstration, or sit-in. And he would be told why: that they knew what he had done, that SNCC did not tolerate that kind of behavior, and that because of his actions, he was exiled permanently. I spoke with the two black staff members I trusted most in our project. Another SNCC member offered to beat Y up, which I opposed. We were publicly a non-violent group, and I didn't want to excuse or encourage violence, even with someone who had violently assaulted me. I was not a complete believer in non-violence; I thought it was okay to defend yourself if someone tried to kill you. But I did not – and still don't – believe in choosing violence when your life is not immediately under threat. I strongly believed in the movement's commitment to non-violence in all its activism. Someone agreed to tell Y what we had decided.

As far as I know, our male SNCC members did not beat him up. Y never showed up at another SNCC event during the next eight months that I was in Arkansas. When my boyfriend arrived two months later, he also wanted to confront the attacker, but I dissuaded him. I wanted to put it in the past, with no further attention wasted on Y. And so it was, as far as I know.

This experience within Arkansas SNCC, of creating a community response to personal violence, has stayed with me throughout my life. It has reinforced my belief that turning to the law must always be a later response, if at all. Not the first resort. The first strategy should always be to think about the victim, the community, and the healing process. With reflection and discussion, I think we can often strategize a non-violent approach, even when confronted with violence.

I soon felt personally safe again in Little Rock. I changed my behavior around men of any race who I didn't know by not being alone with them. I kept the story to myself for almost fifteen years. I didn't speak publicly about the incident or our office's response to it. It didn't completely disappear into the past – I carried the memory of the rape and the response with me, even though I didn't know how to talk about either of them. I didn't want my story to feed into racist perceptions of black male-white female relationships. And, like most women, I felt some kind of shame and responsibility for what had happened. Why hadn't I fought harder, screamed louder? Why had I let him into my room? Had I led him on when I danced with him earlier?

One part of me knew that I didn't want to spend my whole life pretending that I had never been raped. How could I share the complexity of my experiences that night? Only twenty-five years later, when I was teaching a course at UC-Santa Cruz on Women's Health Activism, did I first discuss the rape in public and describe how we dealt with it during that spring in 1965.

PART III

SOCIAL LOCATION PAINS

CHAPTER 14

THE ONE WHO IS BORN
ON SATURDAY

onald and I had met in 1962, shortly after Al Rosanes came to Wellesley to recruit me to the Boston Action Group. He was still Donald then. In the early 1980s he became Kwame, after Ghanian President Kwame Nkrumah, but also the Akan meaning: "one who is born on Saturday." When I first met Don, he was working at a frame shop, making woodcuts and taking beautiful black-and-white photos. He was creative, "alive," and interesting. He was also a socialist, an admirer of Marcus Garvey and W.E.B. DuBois, an activist, as cute as could be, eleven years older than me, neat as a pin, and ardently interested. The combination had been hard to resist. Aside from his charming ways, he seemed to know all the latest everything about contemporary black culture: especially music, literature, and art.

Don introduced me to jazz, which was, and still is, his basic musical love. For me, it's still close to the top, vying with Motown, blues, and new forms of classical music. I absorbed his enthusiasm for the rhythm, intellect, and urban nightlife associated with jazz. His love affair with this music had started when he left his home city of Haverhill, Massachusetts as an older teenager, first for a stint in the Air Force, spent mostly in Japan, and then to become an artist in Boston in the late 1950s.

Don gave me clues about how to listen to jazz ("Try following one instrument, then follow another.") He brought me to various jazz clubs, where we chatted with the musicians. I met the drummer Roy Haynes (his long-time personal friend), the saxophonists Roland Kirk and John Coltrane, Thelonious Monk, Cecil Taylor, Jimmy Garrison, and other incredible musicians and composers.

On weekends in New York, Don and I would stay in one or another funky apartment belonging to a friend. In the evening, we would visit the Five Spot for the latest music. In Boston, we'd go to an early show at the Jazz Workshop or Storyville and hope to be able to stay for a free second show as well. I always felt a little dizzy and out of place as the white girlfriend in a black milieu where sexual *entendres* and offers of drinks and marijuana were common.

We also bonded over reading African American history, fiction, and poetry. We would watch almost anything on television or at the movies that was about people of African descent. We saw Nichelle Nicholls as Lt. Uhura of the Starship Enterprise and Bill Cosby in *I Spy* on television, but our real heroes were in the movies, with dramatic acting and more serious portrayals of racial issues. We went to every film with Sidney Poitier, Ruby Dee, Brock Peters, Claudia McNeill, Abby Lincoln, or James Earl Jones.

Donald had a library of several hundred books. He had a subscription to *Freedomways*; we jointly subscribed to *The Black Scholar*, beginning with its inaugural issue. In Harvard Square, we would pick up the black cultural magazines and broadsides that came and went. I read most of Don's library; together we purchased new works by African American authors as soon as they appeared. Through my relationship with him, I was learning more of the names and absorbing more of the ideas of leaders of the African American community, from the early days of slavery to the present moment. I was enjoying reading history for the first time.

Don also knew lots of visual artists, especially black ones, some of whom he met while studying at the Museum School at the Boston Museum of Fine Arts. Our closest friends were the painter Richard Yarde, and his (white) wife Susan, a poet. Don and I went to art openings, wandered in museums, and visited artists in their studios.

It was as if I suddenly had a guide to an intellectual and cultural world that had always been near me but had been shut away – not only in my youth, but also while in college, where I had been taught only from the white canon. While in the movement, I had been exposed to soul, blues, and gospel as well as religion, social interaction, food, and manners, but I realized there was so much more to learn, including about black life in the north, of which I was quite ignorant.

Donald had dropped out of college after one year to join the Air Force during the Korean War. He spent six months in the Philippines as part of a boxing team, but quit after being knocked down a few times. He became a clerk typist and transferred to Japan for the rest of his three years in the service. There he enjoyed himself and managed to get addicted to heroin. Coming back to Boston in the late fifties, he avoided a worse habit by getting acute Hepatitis C from a dirty needle. In the hospital, he was detoxed (no choice) and decided to stay away from opiates permanently.

By 1958, Don was in art school, but he never graduated. I think money may have been the issue, or maybe he thought he had learned all he wanted and needed to know. He had no academic degrees beyond high school. He would never have access to the privileges I had from being white and from coming from a middle-class family, where my parents had been able to save enough to send me to college without a scholarship.

He was comfortable and direct around whites with whom he shared political and cultural interests, maybe from growing up in the predominantly white world of Haverhill, then spending time in Japan while in the military, and finally being in the world of the arts and culture. He made strong distinctions between white people he could be friends with and those who were racists, whether overtly anti-black or more subtly so.

When I went to Arkansas to work for SNCC in early 1965, at a time that was still early in our relationship, I needed a breather from Don. I was having doubts about being his girlfriend and some part of me thought that if I went South, our relationship would fade away. I was wrong about the fade-away part, however, because two years later in 1966, we were married.

Even though he often said how much he disliked the South because of the dangers and overt evil of white people there, Don quit his job in May, 1965, and arrived in Arkansas the next month. I felt irritated at him for coming. This was my world, and I didn't really want to share it with him. As it turned out, he took beautiful photos of the people he worked with and did a good job at outreach and organizing, too. He was popular with the other SNCC workers and formed friendships that lasted for many years. He worked almost exclusively in West Helena and Forrest City, a few miles from Mississippi and 100 miles from my home base in Little Rock. We saw each other only three or four times during the three months preceding our joint return to the Boston area in September, 1965. I adjusted to the fact that, as a black man with a deep sense of history and culture and great social skills, he might have been more valuable to our project than I was—though I had been there longer, had more southern organizing experience, and managed the movement of materials throughout the state. He was a northerner through and through, but he belonged in a way that I didn't and never would.

Within a month of our return to the north, we began living together on River Street in Cambridge. Everything was relaxed, except for the fact that our landlords, who lived downstairs, thought we were married when we weren't. Don had a job as an outreach worker for a settlement house jobs program in the South End neighborhood of Boston. I was finishing my course work at Brandeis. We pursued our cultural interests together. The following spring, I wrote my master's thesis on how SNCC managed its internal disputes. For field notes, I used my detailed letters, which I had at first sent to Don and, after he arrived, to my friend and sister student Barbara Carter. Soon I would be getting ready for my qualifying exams so I could start work on a dissertation, the topic of which was still a mystery to me.

Don and I started talking about having a child together. We each thought the other would be a good parent, and we seemed to have common ideas about how to deal with racial issues, culture, and socialization. His brother Gerald was living in Mexico with his white wife, her two white children, and their common daughter, Sona. They later had three more children, all born in the little town of Zihuatanejo, where Gerald lived for the next fifty years until his death in 2017. Don and I had no plans to leave the country, as Gerald and Sally had done in their effort to escape American racism. We thought we could manage to live together in Boston without too much race trouble, since we were already doing it. It seemed important and helpful to get married if we were going to have a baby. We didn't want our interracial child to be "illegitimate" in any way. Despite my growing feminism, I thought it would be best for our son or daughter to have both parents with the same last name on the birth certificate.

We married in October, 1966, at our new apartment on Pearl Street between Central Square and the Charles River. Ben Grinage, a self-ordained Baptist minister from Pine Bluff whom we both knew from SNCC, drove up for a few days to officiate. Our guests were a mixture of family, friends, and connections from my graduate school life and the movement.

Don's father, John, had been in the Negro Baseball League, traveling frequently from and to the Shaw home in Haverhill. He and Geneva, Don's mother, had formally divorced when Don was only ten but had lived separately for many years before. My own father had died when I was twenty. This left our mothers to bless our marriage. Instead of blessing it, however, they both opposed it. My mother took one low road and told me she was sure my deceased father would have disapproved because our child would suffer. Donald's mother found another low road and maintained that I was just using her son while I was in graduate school, and that I was certain to divorce him once he had supported me through my education. As it turned out, I *would* divorce him, but not for the reasons Geneva had in mind.

Despite their misgivings, both our mothers came to the wedding, where they looked at us (and each other) with suspicion. My mother, Ruth, had remarried and brought her husband, Ben, who was, as usual, chatty and friendly with everyone. Geneva came with her daughter Eunice and son-in-law Calvin. Eunice and I were already close friends, a friendship that lasted until her death from early Alzheimer's in 2004. Over the years, all the younger women in the extended Shaw family, whether ex-girlfriends or lovers who happened to have children by either Don or Gerald, became friends – especially with Eunice and her children – and all our children did, too. Calvin and I also became friends. A socially conservative banker, he considered me to be the most "normal" of the extended Shaw family, by which he meant I had the most stable middle-class job.

Back at the wedding in 1966, about thirty people crowded into our combined living-dining room—our friends from SNCC, members of my graduate student cohort, several sociology faculty from Brandeis, Don's best friends, and our mothers. Claude Weaver, another civil rights friend, and Richard Yarde, Don's best friend, stood next to him for the ceremony. My brother Bob gave me away. With the help of our friends, Don and I supplied the food. A female friend of his made my wedding dress.

When I look back on the setting and the way our friends supplied the food and drink, I realize that we never seriously contemplated a big wedding, and no one in either of our families offered to help with one. I wore a white dress with lavender-lined sleeves made by a female friend of Don's, and he wore a suit. We included no religious aspect. (My stepfather, Ben, appeared as a friend with the right legal credentials to sign the form.) We knew the event was more about our legal status as parents for our still unconceived child than it was about true love forever. We needed witnesses, and we wanted our supportive friends and family there.

The SNCC and civil rights movement contingent had arrived early to visit, and began drinking before the actual ceremony. No one was really drunk, but to my distress and embarrassment, Ben Grinage forgot some of his ministerial lines. Once the ceremony was over, we had a party.

Everyone was keyed up by the wedding and the marriage. While our mothers were anxious in their own ways, our friends expressed a different kind of excitement. Don and I knew that the marriage would have been difficult or illegal in most southern states. *Loving v. Virginia*, which legalized mixed-race marriages in my own home state, was not decided by the Supreme Court until June 12, 1967, a year after our wedding. Alabama enforced its racial purity laws until 1970 and only removed an anti-miscegenation clause in its state constitution in 2000. Going against these laws was part of the appeal of the wedding and our marriage. I felt both surprise and appreciation that all my professors were supportive. I hadn't known how they would feel, and thought some might take my mother's view that even though activism was a good thing, getting married and having mixed-race children were two allied but equally bad moves.

I was so excited and distracted that I forgot to eat anything beyond the traditional slices of wedding cake during the six hours of visiting, services, and celebrating.

I remember being incredibly hungry as soon as the last person left. After getting over my shock that I had missed all the great food, I made myself an American cheese sandwich. Exhausted but happy, Don and I went to bed.

CHAPTER 15

MOTHERHOOD AND PERSONHOOD

The two years between marriage and motherhood remain in my memory as a series of peaceful moments. Graduate school went well. I found a dissertation topic, the hospital management of childbirth, and plunged into the research by spending a year at a public-private hospital, where I compared the treatment of private and public patients (paying special attention to race). Some side trips to other hospitals and a midwifery service helped my comparative analysis. Donald and I got along fine, sharing the work of our common household, doing a little political work, and continuing our cultural explorations. Not bad for the start of our life together.

It took me a while to get pregnant, but finally, in early 1968, I began to miss my periods. The doctor calculated that the baby would be born in late September. I was still doing my field research, but put off telling the staff at the Boston Lying-In Hospital, where I spent most of my time. One day in April, I was watching a birth and felt faint. I had to leave the delivery room and sit in the hall. From then on, the staff teased me repeatedly about my choice of research. Had I selected it to prepare myself? No, I was

just interested in how hospitals handled birth and death.
I had a relatively easy pregnancy—no serious morning sickness that couldn't be cured by five or six saltines. I remained healthy throughout. At the time, one of the medical goals of pregnancy management was to keep one's weight down and gain a maximum of fifteen to twenty pounds. I followed this guide religiously, eating probably the healthiest diet I had in years.
A light smoker, I had a few cigarettes a day throughout my pregnancy. The only thing I had heard about the effects of smoking on pregnancy was that the child of a smoker was likely to be a little lighter in weight. That sounded fine to me, because I was watching lots of births at the Lying-In Hospital and knew that big babies were harder to deliver. Towards the end of the pregnancy, I concluded that smoking probably wasn't such a good idea, but at least I hadn't smoked *too* much. And I planned on natural childbirth and Lamaze preparation, so I decided that I would get my smoking down to one cigarette a day and then not smoke at all during labor—mostly so I'd have enough breath to manage my contractions. I managed this and quit smoking on the day of our baby's birth. It was much harder to smoke when she was little, because my hands were usually too engaged to light a cigarette. This made keeping myself from starting again a lot easier. If the urge got too strong, I would take a few puffs of a joint. Then I'd lose my desire to smoke anyway. A perfect transitional technique. There were no prenatal instructions on alcohol, other than the advice to women who were having trouble conceiving that they should drink before sex in order to relax more! As a light drinker, I don't think I consumed much alcohol and only an occasional, small amount of marijuana.

In 1968, the film *Rosemary's Baby* had just come out. In the film, Mia Farrow plays a young woman impregnated by Satan. She and I had the same haircut.

Although friends told me not to see the film—it would

scare me too much—with interest, I went to a screening. Other than having people stare at me (did they think I had cut my hair like hers on purpose?) and my feeling of pride that some people thought I looked like Mia Farrow, I wasn't scared at all about my own pregnancy. Instead, I worked on continuing to look like Mia Farrow: thin but pregnant, with good posture and a pixie haircut.

I remember that sweltering pregnant summer well. I was hot, and tired of being pregnant. Sleeping was more and more uncomfortable. My baby stretched its elbows and feet in an increasingly crowded uterus. I could see and feel the movements across my abdomen, which by now seemed bigger than the rest of my torso. I continued to be as active as I could. I knew that once the baby was born, it would be harder to do things. I had no idea just how much harder it would be. It was mid-August. The Delano Grape Boycott was in full swing, and Cambridge activists were in full support.

I put on my favorite pregnancy dress, a loose Marimekko with dark green and black stripes. I drove to the nearby Stop and Shop (it was too hot to walk) to join a picket line advising people not to buy grapes. I picketed for two hours. I think I looked like a watermelon—perhaps I was a walking advertisement for a good alternative to a grape feast.

A month later, as I was trying to decipher some field notes, I realized I had gone into labor. Don came home from work and took me to the same hospital where I had been doing research for the last two years. More teasing and some general surprise came from some of the nurses I knew. "Even after all your research, you still wanted to come here?"

"Yep. I'm lucky, I know what to expect."

My knowledge didn't stop me from having painful contractions, despite my prepared childbirth training. It did keep me from being shocked or angry when I was told I had to have an enema, couldn't eat until after the birth, and had to be shaved of all my pubic hair.

Early in the morning of September 28, after about a twenty-hour labor with fifteen hours in the hospital, our child was born. Don wasn't allowed in the delivery room—that sort of thing came later, after the women's movement pressed hard for changes in how birth is handled. I saw him soon after. We had a little girl. We were now parents, with all the challenges and changes that would entail.

Naturally, we both thought our's was the cutest baby ever born. She was certainly cuter than all the babies with no hair and either pink or pale white faces in the nursery. She came out with a full head of thick black hair, a warm skin tone, and beautiful black eyes. She was a little scrunched up in the face for the first day, but that smoothed out soon. Six pounds, ten ounces, and 100% healthy, as far as I could tell.

Later that day, I called my mother to tell her that the baby had arrived. She was happy and perhaps relieved to hear that I'd made it through the delivery okay. She told me she'd be up to help when I was ready and back home. Eventually, she did come for a week, making me delicious custards, doing laundry, shopping, and carrying Gwen around while I got some sleep.

In 1968, no one knew before the birth what sex the baby would be. We had baby names ready to go: for a girl, she would be "Gwendolyn" for Gwendolyn Brooks and "DuBois" for W.E.B. DuBois. (If she'd been a boy, his first name would have been Malcolm with the same middle name.) I don't remember wishing for either sex, although I think I felt some relief that the baby was a girl. I thought I could relate to a girl a little better, since I had been one all my life.

I called my mother again, and this time I shared Gwendolyn's name and its origins. After a few verbal sounds of agreement, Mom wanted to know where "our" side of the family was in this naming. Why weren't we also represented? It hadn't occurred to me that she would want a Klarberg or a Stoller memorialized until she said it. I couldn't think of any famous or inspirational white person I wanted to name Gwendolyn after. No one came to mind who had the stature of the African American intellectuals and activists that we had picked. We wanted Gwendolyn to know through her name some of the values we admired. I felt that it would have been disloyal to my values, and to the life she was about to live, to give her the name of a white person. But I could see my mother's point, and I felt both guilt and a kind of self-erasure. I knew my cells biologically had contributed to Gwendolyn. So in a certain way, she was more my child than anyone else's, even if her genes and heritage derived from many others. I had also heard that in Jewish tradition, you are encouraged to name a child after a deceased family member. Not that my parents had done that with any of their three children: Nancy Elaine, Robert Nathan, and Peter James. Bob's "Nathan" was shared with a living uncle. And my mother didn't even have a middle name.

Since we had given Gwendolyn the names of two powerful black people, I concluded that for my mother's first grandchild, we should add a name from her side of the family. Though my father had died a few years before, I couldn't work in his names, but we did add "Ann" for my father's mother, Anna. By the time we left the hospital, the birth certificate listed: "Gwendolyn Ann DuBois Shaw."

From the moment of her birth, Gwendolyn's identity was being constructed not only by the broader society, but also consciously (and with attendant excitement and anxieties) by her two parents. While observers might try to categorize her as part of a "race," we were already telling her, even through her name, some of the traditions we wanted her to know and hopefully to honor.

CHAPTER 16

THE 24-HOUR DAY

After three days, a normal Boston hospital stay in 1968, Gwendolyn and I returned to the apartment Don and I shared in Cambridge at 118 Pearl St. When we moved in two years before, I hadn't given much thought to how we would live there with a child. The main attractions had been its easy location for public transit, high ceilings, and golden oak floors. Built in 1910, the house was now painted a beautiful deep red. I had felt I was living in a wonderful space, but with a third person in the apartment, I began to assess the rooms differently. The three-story duplex home had been broken into six apartments, three on each side. Our first-floor apartment included a former front parlor, a middle room, and a kitchen, arranged in a shotgun, walk-through fashion. We used the former parlor as a large living room, with a bay window and a non-working fireplace. We used the middle space as a dining room. Someone had built a small sleeping space with glass doors behind the fireplace. Perhaps this had once been part of a downstairs hallway. The kitchen, directly behind the middle room, had just enough space for the basic appliances, and our yellow laminate-top table and its four vinyl chairs. Soon after Gwendolyn's birth, we managed to squeeze a washing machine into the kitchen too. Off the kitchen, there was a small back hallway leading to the building's trashcans in the backyard, shared with the other five apartments. A tiny bathroom completed our home.

For the first few months, we kept Gwendolyn's crib in the middle room. She liked to hang out in the evening, going to sleep at eleven or midnight, then waking to nurse at three or four in the morning before sleeping another few hours. I never seemed to get enough sleep. (Later, when she began to sleep regularly for more than five hours at a time, I realized that I had been in a half-conscious daze for months.) During the day, the only time to catch up on my sleep was whenever she slept. When she was awake, she always seemed to need to be fed or changed. If there was a minute when I wasn't doing that, what about eating my own lunch or doing the laundry or actually making supper? Gradually I learned that almost any household task can be done with one hand, while holding a baby in the other. I bought an accordion-fold canvas sling that I looped over my right shoulder and then slipped Gwendolyn into its seat, just above my left hip. I could then also use my left hand for a few balancing gestures when needed.

Donald's and my parenting patterns set in quickly: I did just about everything that was connected to taking care of Gwendolyn, while he continued his cleaning and dishwashing roles as before. I did the shopping and cooking too. (At this time, he still didn't have a driver's license.) When he was home from work, he'd also play with Gwen, take photos, and be the doting dad. At first, I hardly noticed the difference between the lengths of our workdays. My participation in more of the tasks of childcare (washing clothes, cleaning up, changing diapers, night-time responding, pediatric visits) made some sense, since

I was home most of the time, while he had to be out of the house at 8 and got back home at 6 during the week. The option of having her dad handle the 3 a.m. feeding completely was not available because I was nursing.

At first, I would wake Donald to get him to bring Gwendolyn to the bedroom for me to breastfeed. Sometimes she'd be wide-awake and restless. Another time, someone would have to change her diapers, and maybe even her pajamas too. She might have trouble getting back to sleep. While waking up and leaving your bed, walking twenty feet to pick up a baby, then bringing her to bed (or nursing her in the rocking chair in the living room) and afterwards returning her to her crib may sound like some minor motions that could be repeated in a half-awake state, for me, the process was exhausting.

I began to ask: "Should I ask Donald or do it myself?" "Should I change her clothes?" "Nurse in the living room in the rocking chair? Bring her to the bed, then get back up and put her in her crib again? Or should I ask Donald to do some of this?" Sometimes I'd bring Gwendolyn back to our bed, where I might slump back on the pillows or lie down to nurse. Late-night nursing took at least a half hour, smack in the middle of what had been my normal sleep time, but often it took longer. Then if Gwen had fallen asleep in our bed, I had three choices: ask Donald to take her back to her crib, do it myself, or just keep her in bed with us. Keeping her in bed meant less room, and also violating the 1960s pediatric dictum that doing so was unsafe.

My attempts to get Donald to do any of the late-night work that bracketed the nursing didn't last long. Soon he just slept, while I got up. After the third failure in a row (in the first month!) I gave up. I can see now that my later marital difficulties began then, with the shock of a 1960s political radical suddenly trying to be a dutiful mother living on a limited budget in a nuclear family. I knew a lot about the institutional management of contemporary American births for the benefit of medicine, but I knew nothing about how the accepted organization of motherhood could so totally shut down my political, social, and intellectual life.

The differences in our late-night responsibilities represented only one part of my parenting frustrations. Although I was still a graduate student on my continuing fellowship, I suddenly had no time or place to study or write. Even when I could grab fifteen minutes to look at my field notes, the dining table – where I'd done my previous writing – was covered with baby things. Balancing a notebook while nursing or holding a sleeping baby wasn't so easy either. I *could* read while nursing. Wow, that was great! An hour later, I didn't know what I'd read. It was impossible to write my usual marginal notes without returning Gwen to some sleeping location (the sofa? our bed? her crib?). "Uh-oh, I forgot, she's sleeping and it's my chance to do the laundry. Or should I take a nap myself? Oh no! What about my thesis?" In addition, I was doing five or six hours more a day of work than Donald was. I worked all day at home, then all evening, and again in the middle of the night.

Within a month of Gwendolyn's arrival in our household, I decided that the public myth of blissful motherhood was in private reality a system of 24-hour servitude. I knew I was supposed to love this, but how could I like these unending duties and the elaborate social rationale telling me I should do all of the childcare *and* the bulk of the housework myself when a healthy, active adult sat next to me reading a book, watching TV, or sleeping? No wonder women have postpartum depression. It isn't just the hormonal changes: it's the second (and third) shift! And it wasn't just the work that made it so depressing and infuriating, it was also the realization that others thought – and said – that I was supposed to enjoy, or at least accept, my 24-hour job.

In 1968, however, my complaints fell mostly on deaf ears. Even my own ears were a little deaf to the problem. One part of me complained, but another part thought that this was just "the way it is." I thought my departure from my "career" in order to live an extended domestic workday would probably continue until Gwendolyn was "in school," a magical calendar moment that would occur in five or six years. Then I would be able to work, to think, to be the professional or activist that I wanted to be. Little did I realize that even when I had a regular full-time job, not just Donald but almost everyone else as well would expect me to do the invisible work of the second shift at home. Somewhere inside, I was probably also modeling myself on my mother, who cared for three – not one! – small children and who still "puttered" in the kitchen in the evening when we were in high school and she held a full-time job. The contradictions between my expectations and reality were hard to accept.

Ah yes, dear reader, as you may have guessed, this was the beginning of the end of my happy marriage. It was also, co-incidentally, the historical moment of the rise of second-wave feminism, a wave that poured over me soon after Gwendolyn's birth and which I attempted to ride in a thoughtful manner. Feminist analysis made my domestic situation harder to accept, but it was not an easy match. Most of the most mainstream feminism of the late 1960s seemed narrowly constructed, mimicking the language of civil rights but not incorporating the diversity of women's lives (including mine) and the complexities of poverty, wealth, culture, citizenship, and racism into the analysis and strategies for change. As a white woman married to a black man, I disliked much of what I read and found the simple phrases like, "Just ask him to do it," inappropriate to my situation. The call to leave any man who didn't do his share was fine for those without children, and as a woman with an inter-racial child, such a decision seemed even more difficult.

The unequal division of labor continued to bother me. A fair division of labor, in my mind, would have been each of us working the same number of hours in a day. The fact that so many of mine were unpaid made them invisible in a traditional analysis of work. It was feminism that helped me see that part of my problem was not being able to articulate why I felt so unfairly treated.

I realize there were other sources beyond the unequal division of labor that contributed to the end of my marriage (or perhaps it was "my failure at marriage"). For example, there was my childhood induction into equal rights and the reinforcement of those beliefs while I was in the movement. My childhood nickname, "Stonewall," was given me for my tenacity and refusal to quit at anything: wrestling, tree climbing, hiking. In my marriage, this meant that I wouldn't give up easily on getting my partner to do his share. I didn't want to give up on my own rights either, or the marriage itself. I was tenacious, but could I be tenacious about everything I wanted, even when those wants conflicted?

I had been encouraged to critique social rules and roles by my parents. My college logic courses and my childhood induction into rationalism encouraged me to think that one should do what logic demands. Didn't the logic of equality in the movement demand equal sharing at home, as well as in the street and at work?

I knew I wasn't raised to be either subservient or overworked. I wondered, though, if some of my anger at being expected to work the 24-hour day while my husband relaxed came from a sense of privilege that I had inherited as an educated white person. As a white person in the movement, I hadn't minded being in the back row when the press came. I didn't mind leadership from African Americans. That made sense. But in the movement, we were all working just as hard as we could, whether we were black or white. Now as a parent, I couldn't accept that a black man's suffering from racism could justify his unconscious sexism. I couldn't accept the idea that a woman should work longer and harder than a man simply because she gave birth and/or nursed *their* baby. I couldn't accept doing more at home than Donald. Or perhaps I should say, doing *so much more*. Every day.

That was looking at our situation through the lens of equality. Our different views and approaches to parenthood could also be read another way: culture clash.

I came from a white middle-class family with two parents, while Donald's mother struggled to get by and her Aunt Sally, born free but before the end of slavery, helped her to raise her three children. According to family lore, Geneva's husband, John, had simply stopped coming home from the Negro Baseball League Tour when Donald was about six. Geneva was already the primary parent and Aunt Sally the secondary parent, and from 1937 until the mid-fifties when the last child left home, the two women did everything. The boys, Donald and Gerald, were encouraged to stand out in sports and school, while the youngest child, Eunice Joanne, was encouraged to look pretty and become a teacher –both of which she did. She was also taught to cook and keep a nice home. It's not surprising that Donald and I came to parenting with very different ideas of who should do what and why. It was natural to him that the women, or a woman, of the household should care for the children. And I believe that he was proud that he was a present father. He was home every night after work and put his salary in our joint account. (I was still on my fellowship and contributed almost half of our income.) He did half the general housework and made sure our apartment was neat and beautiful. He was gentle, almost never got angry, and played with Gwen whenever he was home. He just didn't do diapers, laundry, any other baby care, or get up at night.

Although I had just become a mother, I didn't want to lose my sense of myself as a person with a career. In my pre-motherhood fantasy, I would start working part-time when Gwendolyn was a few months old and then expand my professional schedule month by month as she got older. I thought that during my year at home after her birth, I would analyze my dissertation data and write up my thesis. Then I'd get a research job and balance it out with activism. Donald would continue working in job development in the black community, and Gwendolyn would soon be in nursery school, kindergarten, and first grade. It seemed that this was a reasonable schedule. (In fact, it took me four more years to finish my thesis and get my doctorate, a time frame that I thought was incredibly slow, but which I later realized to be unusually quick for a woman who married and had a baby during graduate school in the mid-sixties. My tenacity was helpful in that area at least. Finishing a dissertation at all was a big accomplishment for a woman at that time, even without children!)

When Gwendolyn was about three months old, I got a tiny job as a research assistant for my favorite professor, Everett Hughes. He didn't really expect much, just a few hours a week of literature review, which I could do at the Harvard library about ten blocks from our house or from books that I checked out and articles I copied. There was no Internet to access from home (or anywhere else). I was also supposed to go to Brandeis and meet with him one day a week for an hour to discuss our project.

How would I manage my child care? Donald had a full-time job. There were no day care centers nearby. The ones I had heard about sounded more like parking lots for little ones. Baby-sitting was paid for by the hour. At that time, we were carless. (A friend had borrowed our car and totaled it, though fortunately with no harm to himself.) Traveling to Brandeis took about an hour each way by public transportation. Since I was breastfeeding Gwendolyn, but knew nothing about pumping and saving milk except that it was a lot of work and very messy, I couldn't imagine being away from home and baby for more than three or four hours. (The first home-use electric breast milk pump wasn't invented until 1991.) The cost of public transit back and forth to the university and the baby sitter together used up all of my pay. Something was definitely wrong with this picture. Was I actually working for free?

How did other women in graduate school manage? Some had no children and could get some money from fellowships or teaching – as I had before Gwendolyn was born. Several women I knew were married to men who had good jobs as academics or in other professions. All my white women friends were married to white men with middle class jobs (and, I realized later, most came from money and married money). My closest graduate school friend, Barbara Carter, who was Gwendolyn's godmother, was black. She wasn't married, and as far as I know, she has never married. During this period when I was a new mother, she had a fellowship and then got a tenure track job at Spelman College. Later, she was a dean at the new University of the District of Columbia. Although she occasionally got involved with a man, she never had children. She was sympathetic to my situation when Gwendolyn was little, but neither her solutions nor those of my white friends worked for me. My other black women friends with little children stayed home with family or welfare support until their children were old enough for some kind of day care or school.

It seemed that while Gwendolyn was a young baby, I just couldn't get ahead of the curve. I wouldn't be able to make enough money to make working worthwhile. I decided to wait a while until I finished nursing – or some good job showed up.

In the summer of 1969, when Gwen was eight months old, I was handed a summer school job teaching an Introductory

Sociology course at Babson Institute, an undergraduate business school in Wellesley. Every student had to take a social science class as part of his major (there were no women); some chose the quick and dirty plan of summer school to get through to their degree more quickly.

Before starting work, I had to overcome my first significant babysitting challenge as a working mother. Donald was looking for a job, but I couldn't get him to be the "baby sitter." So I found a neighbor who watched Gwen while I was gone. The cost of the baby sitter and transportation was just barely covered by the salary: $900. I rushed out and back every day to keep the costs of the sitter as low as possible, and to get back before her next appointment.

The students were in class somewhat against their will, just as I was. We were both forced to read an incredibly boring textbook. I prepared carefully outlined lectures based on the text, mimicking what I had experienced in college. I gave them a test every Friday and corrected their 28 papers over the weekend. They tolerated me pretty well during my six weeks of pretense that I was an actual sociologist, not just a graduate student who had never taught a course and was only one chapter ahead of them. Even though the class met right after lunch, most of them stayed awake most of the time. I think I passed all but one student.

This was probably the most boring job I ever had, but it brought in cash and had a turn-around time of three hours, including teaching and driving (we now had a car). Now that Gwen ate some solid foods, I was nursing her less and could use a baby sitter more. I graded papers while she played and prepared my lectures while she slept. I was able to clear expenses and save a little money.

I knew that soon Donald, Gwen, and I would be leaving the United States. We had been saving for the past two years, and almost had enough for our plane tickets and cash to last for a year. In my fantasy, I would work on my thesis when I had time, or wait until I got back. Then, I vowed, I would finish the thesis and get a "real job." Donald could go back to his job development work, and everything would be easy. Our plan was to fly to Zihuatanejo, Mexico, where his brother Gerald lived with his family, visit for a month or two, check out more of Central America, and then take a freighter south to Brazil. We'd stay in Bahia for a while and then wander further in Latin America.

CHAPTER 17

MEXICO AND MOROCCO

We packed up our belongings in August, 1969, and boarded a plane for Mexico City.

After two days in the capital, we took a small plane to Zihuatanejo. There was no international airport and no Ixtapa yet. Those changes that made Zihuatanejo a big resort town were still years in the future. Our eight-seater airplane dipped down into a tiny valley and pulled up on a short runway next to a small office. We were in the center of a palm tree plantation. Gerald and Sally emerged from the trees to meet us and helped us into a taxi, and we traveled the three miles to town.

Located 100 miles north of Acapulco, Zihuatanejo was a little fishing village that had become home to a collection of expatriates from the United States and Europe. Sally and Gerald had been there for three years, supporting themselves on Sally's welfare checks, some low-key smuggling of marijuana to the United States, and buying and selling pre-Columbian pottery and jewelry pieces that were turned up by local farmers.

Our home for the next month would be a two-room house with a palm frond roof on the main town beach. There was a bathroom, a kitchen-living room, and a bedroom. We got our groceries at a small general store, bought meat and fish at a market, and cooked on a small propane stove. At night we used electric lights.

Gerald and Sally were a little out of town, up a hill, where they had been building their own house. When we walked up there through palm, papaya, and banana trees the next day, I was surprised to see there were no full walls in their house. A traditional *palapa* with a palm frond roof and tree trunk supports, the building had waist-high walls around the edge and slightly higher ones inside. The bathroom was an outhouse. The shower was outside. Water came from a well. They cooked on a wood fire and went to sleep at sunset, or used lanterns when it was dark. For transportation, they had their feet and a burro to carry small children and supplies from town.

Our days consisted of going to various beaches, eating local food, hanging out with the family, making friends among the expatriates, and cooking in traditional ways. Sally did all the childcare and housework with the help of her older children, who were now five and eight, while Gerald worked some on the house and carved art pieces. Sally and Gerald's baby, Sona, was almost four, and Sally was pregnant with her next child, Nyanza, who would be born in 1970. Things were peaceful overall, but their life seemed to require a lot of manual work and lots of walking up and down hill, neither of which was I used to. I tried to develop my Spanish, relax, and take my mind off my academic work back in Boston.

On Sept. 26, her birthday, Gwendolyn got sick. At first it just seemed like a little diarrhea, but in a few days, it was much worse. She had a high fever, no appetite at all, and just looked bad. I took her to the local clinic. Sally accompanied me because I had no idea what to do. Local families filled the reception room, waiting to be seen. We were the only gringos. Naturally, everyone stared at us. Sally explained to the receptionist in her rudimentary Spanish that my baby was very ill. After an hour's wait (probably shorter than the average local had to wait), we were taken to an examination room. The doctor decided that Gwendolyn was severely dehydrated and needed a saline infusion.

A nurse came to put the IV in. The needle was large—perhaps sized for an adult, not for a small child—and it was dull! As she tried to insert it, it bent. "Stop!" I yelled. She stopped. I was shaking, Gwen was crying, and Sally was saying, "It's okay, we'll figure it out." I didn't believe her. Another wait ensued.

A different doctor arrived with a different IV kit, one designed for a child. He set up the IV, and we waited in the room while Gwen got some fluids in her. This doctor was part of a national system in Mexico requiring all graduates of medical schools to spend a year in a rural clinic before practicing elsewhere or specializing. He diagnosed Gwen as having a bacterial infection, probably from contaminated water. It would take a few days to get the exact diagnosis, he said, but meanwhile he gave us some antibiotics.

After going back to our house, Donald and I did our best to care for her, but she seemed to get weaker and weaker. I could tell she was losing weight. The pathology report came back in three days, but was inconclusive. I was desperate. It seemed my daughter was wasting away. Sally suggested that I take her to Mexico City. There were doctors there who spoke English, and we could stay at the Casa de los Amigos, run by the Quakers. Somehow, I bundled up Gwen and got on a plane. Donald would come in a day or two.

Exhausted, I brought Gwen to the suggested doctor. He recommended a different antibiotic and sent out for more tests. When Donald arrived he, too, was losing weight. Now I had two patients to care for, and nothing seemed to work. I wanted to go back to Boston, where I knew the health care system. I thought that if Gwen had to be in a hospital, I would feel more confidence there than in this country, where I could barely speak the language.

On the 12th day after Gwen's initial illness, when Donald had improved somewhat, we three boarded a plane. In three hours, we arrived in Dallas, where the World Series played on four TV screens near our gate as we waited for our flight to Boston. Gwen began crying. I couldn't figure out what to do. Then it occurred to me that she was hungry, that the medicine was finally working. Donald bought her a hot dog, which she consumed quickly.

It was the beginning of her recovery. She had lost four pounds—a fifth of her body weight—since we'd arrived in Mexico six weeks earlier. She had been practicing walking before her illness, but now she was set back and did not walk by herself until she was almost a year and a half. Still, she was alive, and we were soon in Boston celebrating.

We'd planned to be away for a year. Now, with a daughter who was soon healthy and two adults who were jobless but had savings, we talked about what we would do next. Donald had always wanted to go to Africa, and this appealed to me as well. So by mid-November, despite concerns from family and friends, we were on another plane, this time to Paris. From there we took a train to Madrid and another to the coast. From there it was a two-hour ferry ride, and we were in Tangier.

It certainly wasn't what I'd expected when I imagined Africa. First of all, it was North Africa, far from the equator. In November it was cold and rainy. Our apartment in Tangier had the beginnings of that winter's mold on the walls and was constantly chilly. Secondly, we were living in a high-rise apartment in a big city. To shop, I replicated my mother's experience of going down four flights of stairs, walking with my daughter in a baby carrier on my back, and then returning home with the supplies. After a few days, though, I calmed down and began to enjoy this new world.

Our friend, gave us travel ideas. We visited Ch'chouen, the hill city with blue painted windows. We planned a bus trip through Meknes, Fez, and Marrakech. Randy encouraged us to go to Ourzazate to visit the Gnaoua musicians. After a month in Tangier, we moved southward, amazed at the elegance of Fez and Meknes. Then we were happily overwhelmed with Marrakech. We decided to stay through December.

At last, for the first time in my life and six years into our lives as a couple, we were living in a country where race was not the primary lens through which we were viewed. Moroccans—indigenous Arabs and Berbers—viewed us more through a continental lens. They saw Donald as an African, perhaps from nearby or from south of the Sahara. He might pass for a Moroccan, or from Western Sahara, southern Algeria, or even Mali. People spoke to him first in Arabic. I was viewed as a French woman married to this dark-skinned African. My tourist-level French reinforced the mistake.

Both men and women remained friendly to us when they learned that we were two Americans. They treated Gwendolyn as the appealing result of our marriage. People seemed to view our marriage and having a child as a sign of happy connection between countries and peoples who once were foes, or colonialist and colonized. On the bus from Meknes, riders passed Gwendolyn from seat to seat and give her cookies to nibble on. It felt so refreshing after our life in the United States and brief time in Mexico, where we were always viewed suspiciously. Before coming to Morocco, I hadn't noticed the racism in Mexico, perhaps because it was so much less than what we had experienced in the United States.

The mixtures of North Africa are ancient, and the many shades of people with mixed European and African ancestry are completely normal. In Mexico, though, it seemed that notions of miscegenation and purity complicated the memory of colonialism. People judged others by skin color and their connections to Europeans, or to the indigenous population. There were terms to describe mestizos, Indians, Europeans. In Morocco, as I saw it then, there were Moroccans and there were people from other countries. Perhaps the emphasis in Islam on accepting all people who are believers, regardless of where they come from, contributed to this inclusiveness. In any case, we felt more welcomed in Morocco than elsewhere in 1969.

Now in Marrakech, in late December, we were living in a studio apartment at the top of a little hotel on the edge of the Jemaa El-Fnaa, Morocco's grandest market. My social role as a mother protected me from much of the sexism so many young foreign women experienced in North Africa. Even the sexism and basic male control of women, so often cited by my Euro-American friends as a North African and Muslim blight, didn't seem to me a simple matter. Nor was it consistently expressed in Morocco. When we went south to the edge of the desert to hang out with Gnaoua musicians, we found that the women were welcome at social occasions and meals. They spoke loudly and often. Nor did they cover their faces—except in the winter cold or during a dust storm, just as the men did.

Although we felt protected from some of the racism we usually encountered, our stay in Morocco did not solve our personal problems. I had given up on trying to do anything related to my temporarily abandoned career. I reminded myself that I was on vacation from "work." Still, I was the American mother of a one-year-old, and I was married to a man who believed a woman should do all the childcare. His attitude aligned with the Moroccan view of a woman's role, but it was not how I saw women's roles. If both adults in our family were supposed to be on vacation, for me it did not allow daily picnics and peaceful wanderings.

I have photos that show Donald carrying Gwendolyn in the back carrier, but I also have my own memories of his leaving our apartment in Tangier or our rooftop studio in Marrakech to go off photographing for hours. I found myself doing the shopping, cooking, clothes and diaper washing, and most of the parenting. I had already absorbed a lot of the domestic work beyond childcare while we were living in Boston. I had slipped deeper and deeper into it while being the nursing mother, and more likely to be at home parent, back in America. In Mexico, Sally had reinforced this idea of what a woman should be doing. Now in Marrakech, I might need to make lunch or prepare dinner, so why not do the shopping, wash up the dishes during the day, and get the laundry done now, while Gwen is sleeping? Just like back home.

Donald's excuse for not taking Gwendolyn out with him when I wanted time for myself in Morocco sounded simple enough: "I just can't photograph and carry Gwendolyn at the same time." But the subtext was that we were in Africa especially for Donald, to give him the deeper pleasure and cognitive awakenings of being in his ancestral homeland. I believed that I should support his exploration of the world around us, since the dominant culture in our birth country had denied and hidden the value of almost all things African. It wasn't that I didn't love Gwendolyn, or enjoy Morocco, or support Donald's project of understanding and artistic documentation. It was just that the way it was put together seemed unfair. I was home doing the dishes and changing the diapers while he was out enjoying the country. That wasn't really what I thought I'd signed up for—I'd imagined a joint exploration of North African culture and politics.

After our return to the United States the following spring, I told my friends, family, civil rights colleagues, and graduate school cohort that Morocco was a place where people treat all shades as a part of the normal range of human variety. I said that perhaps the Moroccan attitude arose from being located between the light-skinned people of Europe and much darker-skinned Africans south of the desert. Referring to Malcolm X's *Autobiography*, I reminded them that Islam emphasizes respect and rights for all people, regardless of color or background. Its philosophy is explicitly opposed to rejecting a person because of skin color or nationality.

At the same time, though, my frustration about my domestic work overload and Donald's lack of respect for my own life goals, which had begun to gnaw at me in Morocco, were escalating in our new Boston apartment, just off the Fenway. By March, 1970, the domestic tension had deepened, and in less than a year it would turn into the crisis of separation and divorce. First, however, I had to practice interracial parenting, and I had a new job to explore.

CHAPTER 18

LEARNING BALANCE AND STABILITY

From the time I got pregnant, I was told that my own child would be a member of the African American "race," a race legally, socially, genetically, and unalterably different from my own.

Her black and Jewish grandmothers each saw Gwendolyn as "really" part of her side of the family. Geneva knew Gwendolyn to be a black child no matter what I might do as a parent, and my mother was convinced that Gwendolyn was her direct descendent through her own daughter. She would always be a Stoller and a Jew, "even if" she was black. I think for my mother, Gwen's African American identity was a kind of secondary characteristic, but her femaleness and her being a member of our family was the deepest identity. In my mother's mind, all the inheritable characteristics of my lineage, whether genetic or social, flowed through me to Gwendolyn.

Still, I fielded questions from outside our families, either directly or indirectly, about to my "right" to be Gwendolyn's parent. A person might accept that I had given birth to her, but they might still ask me what I knew that would be of use to her as a black youth or adult. Not only strangers, or Black Power separatists, asked this question—at various times, I even asked it of myself. Could I ever be a thoroughly good parent? Could I ever understand what her life was like, or would be like? In a country where racial imputation is one of the key factors in survival and well-being, how could I, an identified member of the privileged group, really be able to assist her in her psychological, social, and emotional survival?

It was October, 1970. Gwendolyn was two years old. We were at a small playground next to the Fenway, two blocks behind our Hemenway Street apartment in Boston. I stood next to the sandbox where Gwen was learning to balance, wobbling along its wooden frame with her arms out to each side.

"Are you stable?" I asked.

"Stable," she said, turning the sound of the word around on her tongue. "Stable....stable!"

I smiled, a little excited. I thought, "stable"—what a great early word for a two-year-old to learn.

A twenty-something white woman in a dark brown wool coat stared back and forth between Gwen and I. What was she looking at? She wasn't friendly. I sensed an attitude of suspicion in her narrowed eyes and tilted head. There was no acknowledgement that we were three people in a single social moment. She was only four or five feet away, but she stared at us as if her stare was invisible to us. Then I got it. She couldn't figure out what the connection was between my daughter and me. Her look said, *Why are these two people together at the playground? What does this white woman have to do with this black child? Is there something illegal going on?*

First, I experienced a beautiful moment of discovery about my child's walking, thinking, learning, and speaking. Seconds later, I was angry at the thought that my daughter and I were the observational subjects of a stranger's racialized construction of human beings. I wanted to look into her eyes and inform her directly that a white woman with wavy, light brown hair can have a honey-skinned child with curly black hair. "Hey, it's okay. All humans are mixtures!" I wanted to deliver a rapid-fire—but friendly ––two-minute lecture to undo the confusions of US categorical thinking about race.

Okay, I could accept that her imagination was limited. It wasn't her fault she grew up here. We are ignorant of who we are, and who we may be. It's our national secret, in which everyone is invested. "Don't tell me and I won't tell you. Let's just absorb our national ideology of color and race."

Even now, 45 years later, most Americans act as if our exclusionary essentialist categories are real facts. Even when we "know" it's not true, even if we want to upend the values ranking which color is best or which race one should cling to, most people "who believe they are white," as Ta-Nehisi Coates writes in *Between the World and Me*, still accept the outlines of the categories. They are embedded deeply in our culture, our language, and contemporary science.

I wanted to tell this woman that the opposite is really the case: Mixtures are the way that inheritance always works, for all humans, even in America! We're no different from Mendel's flowers, or from other beings in the world. That old saying that "there's only one human race" is so much more true than we seem able to acknowledge.

I couldn't bring myself to speak up. Instead, I walked away with Gwendolyn, thinking to myself: "Stable…stable…stable…I have to keep myself balanced. Keep Gwendolyn balanced. We are balanced in the world, in between two falling points."

It's as if we were both walking on a piece of wood, just a few inches wide, at the edge of a sandbox. Gwen was balanced between a drop in either direction. Black? White? Nowhere?

Somewhere? She would have to create the balance herself. Maybe my job was to help her figure out her own way to stability.

Forty-five years later, visiting Gwen in Philadelphia, the word "stable" will come back to me. I will see her father, now going by the name Kwame, grasp his cane to stabilize himself as he complained that his grandson Ben wouldn't walk on the black side of the balance beam that is America's racial heritage.

CHAPTER 19

TROUBLEMAKER IN THE ACADEMY

That spring of 1970, after our return from Morocco, we began with a little money and we both had jobs. I did have time to take Gwendolyn to the playground, to relax, and even to attend some consciousness-raising group meetings. The National Organization for Women had just started a chapter in Boston and I began to attend the meetings. I knew it was time for me to find some work and to make serious progress on my dissertation. With my fellowships ending, I needed paid work.

My primary professor had written to tell me that my ten-page summary of my proposed dissertation, composed on a manual typewriter I found at the apartment we had sublet in Tangier, had some interesting ideas, but too many leaps between the segments of my arguments. I realized that my morning hash smoking had probably created those leaps. It had been clear to me – why hadn't it been clear to others? I would have to lay off the marijuana if I was going to write a dissertation.

Meanwhile, help – and the beginning of my professorial career – was on the way. The chair of my department at Brandeis told me that a Catholic women's college in Boston sought a full-time sociology instructor to start in the fall. The person had to be what is known as ABD (all but dissertation) and able to teach a range of undergraduate courses, probably Introductory Sociology and some other courses that could be negotiated. I went to the interview wondering how a Catholic school could ever hire a radical activist Jew. The interview process itself provided the first of many surprises at the college: the hiring committee had students on it.

The chair of the Sociology Department was a member of the Sisters of Notre Dame, who ran the college. Her order was firmly in support of the current wave of liberation theology championed by Pope John. The college itself was undergoing major changes in student rights. The year before my arrival, students got permission to wear pants to class, forced more open dorm hours, and insisted on participating in hiring in some departments. Some students had dropped out to transfer to less restrictive (non-religious) environments, and others to join the workforce or become hippies or activists. I learned that fall that one of the favorite jokes in the Sociology Department was, "We judge our success by the dropout rate: the more dropouts, the more successful we have been in our critique of capitalism and the role of education."

Everyone seemed to like my background as a civil rights activist. Within a week, I had been hired, and my courses for both fall and spring settled. I would join the rest of the department in teaching the Introductory Sociology course, which turned out to be a global critique of capitalism and its effects on the poor. I would offer my own courses on Family, Deviance, and Race and Ethnicity. Not bad, except that I had never even taken a course on the Family myself.

"No," I told Sr. Marie Augusta. I didn't think I could teach that course.

"Your dissertation is on childbirth!"

"Yes, but it's not about family," I replied. "It's about hospitals and doctors, and how institutions manage women, and the differences between care for the poor and those with money."

"We need someone to teach family. And besides, you can teach it however you want."

"Okay, I'll figure it out." (After all, wasn't the unstated motto of SNCC, "We'll just make it up?")

So began my first course on gender and sexuality, my first full-time naïve fall into academic troublemaking, and alongside all this, my road to lesbianism. Plus I was able to bring my thoughts on racism into all my courses.

To teach the Family course, I decided to take the approach that "family," as a social institution, had four basic functions: control of sexuality and reproduction, socialization, and the management of kinship and inheritance. Socialization and kinship I managed to teach without too much trouble (although I did get into several feminist critiques of patriarchy, which began my academic comparisons of ethnic differences in family culture). My approach to sexuality and reproduction, given my employment by a Catholic college, caused a minor sensation. I had decided to present some of the new media and organizational efflorescence coming out of the sexual revolution of the late sixties, the rise of feminism, and the contemporary women's health movement, within which I situated my work on childbirth.

For the section on sexuality, I had students read anthropological literature on sexual diversity, and I invited speakers from the Daughters of Bilitis (a lesbian organization) and Gay Male Liberation to talk about alternative views of how sexuality might exist outside traditional heterosexual marriage. As part of our study of reproduction, I showed a film that advocated more lenient rules on access to abortion and also supported greater access to birth control. I also shared parts of the first newsprint version of *Our Bodies Ourselves* (*OBOS*), which friends of mine had just produced as part of the women's self-help health movement. The enthusiasm of students for *OBOS* was such that I started a volunteer study group on the book that met after class in an empty classroom. *OBOS* had been modeled on a course format, so each chapter was designed to go with a weekly meeting.

I knew, of course, that the Catholic Church was opposed to homosexuality, but what religion wasn't?

Students responded enthusiastically to my "more interesting course content than a standard family textbook." My pupils invited their friends to guest lectures. In one year, the enrollment jumped from 20 to 110. Sister Marie Augusta Neal, my department chair, invited me to add a new course for my second year of teaching: Sociology of Women. In the third year, I added a course on Women's Health.

News of my course content, however, spread to the more conservative faculty. First, someone complained that our *OBOS* workshop messed up a usually vacant classroom in the evenings, and that students were smoking in the classroom. When Sr. Marie Augusta explained the complaints, I asked what I should do.

"Just clean up," she replied.

In the fall of 1971, I taught the Family course in the largest lecture hall on campus while I planned for my Sociology of Women class for the spring. When the Daughters of Bilitis spoke on female homosexuality, I remember that one of my students asked hesitantly if she could bring her friend to class. "Sure," I said. They sat in the first row, listening intently. Only months later did I realize that her "friend" was probably her lover. Even though I was teaching about lesbians, I thought of myself as completely straight and imagined that everyone I met, unless they had a label on, was also straight. I also recall that the DOB speakers talked primarily about their desire to get married, "just like everyone else." I was shocked. To me, being a lesbian meant critiquing marriage, not yearning for it. It was very educational for me, as well as my students.

A week later, the room was packed for the guest speakers from Gay Male Liberation. This time, however, we had a surprise visitor: Emmanuel's vice president, John O'Brian, a florid layman in his mid-fifties. He told me he was there because he'd been informed that I was having some "controversial" guest speakers and he wanted to hear for himself.

"Of course," I said, both surprised and a little shocked. My view of teaching and academic freedom held that a professor could have any speaker come to class that she could arrange. It made classes interesting, and students then discussed the point of view presented.

O'Brian's presence caused a major flurry of whispers as he fitted himself into one of the desks high up in the back of the lecture hall. He was almost a foot taller and fifty pounds heavier than any of the hundred or so women in the room. The two Gay Male Liberation speakers both spent their time critiquing patriarchy and sexism. One was explicit about marriage:

"I don't want to be part of the sexist patriarchal system where men dominate women. I oppose marriage; it's a patriarchal institution. No one should get married. I love women, but I don't want to dominate them. I love men, too, and I want to learn to be friends with men, not to compete with them. I want to be in an equal relationship."

The students loved these speakers. After the guests and the vice president left, a student announced that she was sorry that the speakers were gay, because she'd love to go out with a guy who thought like they did. Others agreed. I concluded: two highly successful classes about how marriage and family do, or do not, control sexuality. Of course, it didn't end there.

In the spring semester, along with two other less controversial courses, I taught my Sociology of Women class. My texts included *Our Bodies, Ourselves*, which had been published in paperback. Students continued to have a separate time each week to discuss the reading. In mid-semester, though, Sr. Marie Augusta told me to expect to be called to a meeting with some senior members of the faculty to discuss my teaching. I was alarmed. What had I done? We cleaned up after the workshops. No one was smoking in the classroom. The department had approved all my course outlines before I taught the courses. I got great reviews. What could be wrong?

"Just stay calm," was my chair's advice.

"Okay," I thought. After all, it didn't seem like I had a choice. Being called to a critique because I taught about women disturbed me. I had grown up in the fifties, when communism was a public threat and one couldn't use Marx or Engels as a text. Perhaps unsurprisingly, even at Wellesley the faculty had a very dismissive view of socialism. Although many of my Emmanuel Sociology Department colleagues spoke out to critique capitalism, opposed the war in Vietnam, and lauded revolution, none of them had been called in to defend their courses. Reproductive rights and female sexuality, I thought, might be more threatening than communism.

One day I received my official request (my "order" would more accurate) to meet with the faculty review committee. Their concerns were that I had used an unscholarly text, I had allowed students to smoke, and I had encouraged students to use birth control. They requested a meeting the following week where I could respond.

At the meeting, I discovered that the unscholarly text was *Our Bodies, Ourselves*. I explained that it was only one among a number of works that students read and had been encouraged to critique. There was no evidence for the smoking charge, but the birth control charge proved to be the most interesting. I thought they would argue that I was promoting abortion or homosexuality, but these topics might have been just too abhorrent for them to discuss. So they selected birth control education as their target. I discovered that several of the eight people in the room had done detailed readings of *OBOS*, which fascinated me. Two interrogators asked me to interpret certain sentences where women told their stories (all *OBOS* chapters contained a mixture of expert commentary and first-person accounts.) The committee opposed my sharing these passages with my students, but they were obsessed enough to read them in detail themselves.

There was no one in the room to defend me. I felt on my own in the face of an inquisition. My attackers included religious and lay people, including one lay woman who seemed especially incensed. I defended my choices and explained why my approach was appropriate, but I was quite shaken. Then I was dismissed.

As soon as I could, I spoke with Sr. Marie Augusta. I poured out my story, and she tried to soothe me, saying that although it was unusual, this was a promotion or retention committee and they had a right to ask questions.

"What will happen next?" I asked, thinking that this in itself had been horrible enough. She seemed to think that there would be some decision about what I could teach, and also a decision about whether I would be promoted to the position of Assistant Professor. A promotion would entail a raise and a transition to the tenure track. Ordinarily, a person was eligible for the promotion after teaching successfully for a year and having good recommendations. They had "somehow" skipped promoting me last year. I was about to get my doctorate in June, just two months away. I was actually overdue for promotion, according to Emmanuel rules, but I hadn't realized it until now.

Further withholding my promotion (and my raise) would have been a definite punishment and a signal that I would not advance within the College.

Sr. Marie Augusta said that there was a division among the faculty about my teaching. Many people supported me (including her, I realized). "Be patient," she counselled, and offered to tell me more as events unfolded.

As soon as I could, I went to talk with the faculty in my department at Brandeis. They were furious, viewing the case as an infringement on free speech and the rights of faculty. They immediately offered to write a letter of complaint to Emmanuel and to make the situation public, either at the AAUP or the American Sociological Association, where several of them were national leaders. It felt to me like a fight between the Jews and the Catholics. There I was, feeling like an innocent atheist caught in the middle.

I told Sr. Marie Augusta what the Brandeis faculty wanted to do. But she cautioned patience: "This publicity would be terrible for Emmanuel. Academic freedom? A prestigious university graduate program versus our undergraduate college? Think of Catholic education and free speech."

I also let her know that I wanted to tell my students, who I knew would make some kind of public demonstration.

"No, no, wait, wait!" she tells me. She says she's going to talk to the college president about my promotion. I'm beginning to build a more complex picture of Emmanuel. Liberals and conservatives are not divided by Catholic and non-Catholic, nor by religious vs. lay persons. Some of my strongest supporters turn out to be nuns and priests, while two of the people who are most vehemently against my teaching are lay people, a man and a woman.

A month goes by, two months. As the end of the school year draws close, I have heard not a word about my promotion.

Finally, I make an appointment to see the President. I explain how the Brandeis department feels, how they want to make this issue public. I remind her that I have not gone to the press and I have not discussed it with my students. She, too, asks me to be patient. My view is once the summer comes, there will be nothing I can do. Students will be gone, and no one will care what happens in the back rooms of administrative meetings. I let her know my concerns as politely as I can. She asks me to trust her, and tries to assure me with vague promises that something can be done in the summer.

Sr. Marie Augusta tells me that the college president is an ethical person and her word is good. I decide to wait, partly because I don't want so much focus on me – even though I do relish the chance to talk about the ridiculous committee and how interested the students are in feminism and their reproductive rights. I think that Sr. Marie Augusta knows much more about how the church and the college work than I do. I know she likes me and believes in this kind of teaching.

The semester ends with no result and I go home for the summer, wondering if I've done the right thing. I'm somewhat consoled by passing my doctoral defense and being asked in the following week if I'd be interested in having my thesis published by a major scientific press.

In July, I receive a letter from the Emmanuel College President's Office.

"Dear Professor Shaw,
I am pleased to inform you that you have been promoted to the position of Assistant Professor…"

Well done, everyone!
I've won—we've won—with the major costs being some struggle and not getting any significant publicity about a victory.

The students do know the basics of what happened: Although the vice president had nosed around, the courses could continue. They became accepted as part of the evolving educational culture at Emmanuel College. It is a local victory for feminism, for gay visibility, and for women's health and our reproductive freedom. For me personally, I've learned some important lessons as a teacher about techniques of struggle within academia. What I've learned will be useful when I find myself in an even larger struggle eight years later at the University of California.

CHAPTER 20

CREATING CHILD CARE: "THE BEST LAID PLANS OF WHITE WOMEN..."

t would be too simple to describe my time at Emmanuel as if I'd just walked in and become a full-time teacher; some crucial support did make that possible. Not only did I have a great department that valued my mixed past of activism and scholarship, but I also had something that made it possible for me to work at a professional job: real childcare.

In 1970, before I began my job at Emmanuel, good childcare for a working mother was a patchwork thing, depending primarily on other women caring for children in either the mothers' homes or their own. Public childcare was so limited, costly, and low-quality that most women preferred to have their children in their own home or with another woman's family. For poor women, the options were older children, family members, or no supervision at all. In some cases, a woman could bring her child to work, but this also limited the type of work the woman could do. It depressed her wages further because employers felt that she wasn't giving her all to the job. The still-current racialized distribution of childcare, with black women and immigrants caring for the children of white women, reflects these facts, and the way that racism has allowed white women to rest or get better jobs while women of color are relegated to enabling that white woman's life.

One focus of feminist theorizing and organizing in the late sixties was the economic situation of women: unpaid labor in the home, lack of access to good jobs outside of the home, and care for children if a woman was in the paid workforce. In Boston, a chapter of NOW comprised of middle-class white women had begun meeting in 1968. In 1969, the chapter decided to focus its work on creating a childcare center that its members could use. The center would not only make it easier for these highly educated women to work at well-paying jobs, it would also become a model of feminist child development practice and avoid the direct exploitation of poorer women as in-home child caregivers. With these goals, the Boston Children's Center—and my childcare solution —were born.

By the time I arrived at Boston NOW in mid-spring of 1970, the plans for the center were well underway. It would open in late summer in Brookline to serve about for children. In keeping with NOW philosophy, feminism would inform the pedagogy, from teaching techniques to toys. The chapter was also committed to addressing racial discrimination and class barriers. These three interrelated challenges to change – sexism, racism, and class oppression – influenced the goals for financing, hiring, admissions, and governance.

We decided that half the families would pay their children's fees, and the center would recruit this other half from the Massachusetts program that provided childcare payments for women on welfare who were working or going to school to gain work skills. We thought, correctly, that this would bring in more African American children. Teachers would be both white and black. We would find books and visual materials that showed children of different races, and that foregrounded girls and boys in non-traditional activities. Parents would be encouraged to volunteer frequently, both to keep costs down and to transmit our values further to the children's homes. In reality, volunteering proved to be harder for the families on welfare, because they were less likely to have a second parent available or to have cars. These social structural divisions gave some parents a greater sense of ownership and a closer friendship with the teachers, which proved crucial later in the life of the center.

When the Boston Children's Center opened in early September, 1970, Gwendolyn was the youngest child, just under two years, the official starting age. I don't know how the other parents felt, but for me, the center meant a revolutionary change in my experience of motherhood. From 9 a.m. to 3 p.m., longer if I wished, Gwendolyn was in a place that met her basic needs. Because I paid a flat rate for the full day, five days a week, I no longer needed to rush whatever I was doing to get back to keep the costs down or "release" the babysitter because she had other things to do. For the first few months, I felt guilty using my whole time. I wondered if the teachers would actually take care of her properly. And what about all those children around her, all at once – how would she cope? Gradually, I adjusted to the idea that Gwen would be okay without me during the day, and I could have an extra cup of coffee or pick up some groceries before going to pick her up. Eating lunch with a friend after finishing teaching for the day also became all right. I didn't usually have her stay the full day, as many women did with their children. I didn't always need the time, and I just couldn't let go that much. I did adapt, and I depended on the center for the three years that I taught at Emmanuel. I even used daycare in the summer when I was writing my dissertation. Later, it was a key savior for me during my separation and divorce.

I made some friendships at the center, two of which lasted long after the center ceased to be part of my daily life. Linda Green was an African American mom studying accounting and business who had two children: Dawn, who was a few months older than Gwendolyn, and Dana, about a year younger. Our children hit it off, and so did Linda and I. She came from a large family in Dorchester, which adopted us into its celebrations and weekend hangout times. Linda and her kids visited us regularly, too. Later, I brought Dawn with Gwendolyn, Donald, and myself on a visit to Mexico to see Gerald and his family. The Green-Shaw family connection gradually faded after I moved to California, and as Gwendolyn became a teenager who visited less in Boston. During our time at the BCC, though, Linda and I were allies as well as friends.

My other friend from the center was Patty Greenfield, a white and Jewish child development researcher at Harvard. Her children were Matthew and Lauren, but the real relationship here was with Patty, which has lasted for fifty years. We were the two academics in our NOW group who were most interested in studying what we were trying to do at the Center. I was a trained field worker with interests in institutions and race. Patty had studied child development and the transmission of culture in several areas, including Oaxaca, Mexico. Her closest colleague was Jerome Bruner, an internationally famous developmental psychologist. Patty and I decided to get a grant to study the center and the possible changes that our feminist, anti-racist curriculum might create. With permission from the parents, she applied and received a grant for us.

Patty was the principal investigator, I was the field researcher, and she would help me with appropriate observational techniques. We planned to analyze our data together and write it up for publication. As it turned out, the center provided us with more to study than we bargained for.

The first months of our research, however, seemed to go pretty smoothly. We used part of our funds to purchase more supplies for the center so that we could observe how they were used. I watched how boys and girls used the toys and who got what kind of attention from the teachers, and I interviewed teachers and parents. Soon conflict arrived concerning pedagogy and race.

The head teacher was a young white woman (who I'll call Carole) trained in non-authoritative pedagogy and influenced by Montessori technique. She provided lots of choices and open-ended projects for the children, and had a soft-spoken approach to conflict and socialization. Her lead co-teacher was a middle-aged African American former kindergarten and first grade teacher ("Michelle") with a warm demeanor. She knew each child well and was excellent in helping them in cooperative play. Other teachers and trainees came and went, but these were our two core leaders.

A controversy erupted when Michelle brought in some coloring books for the children to use as part of their art activities. Some of the white parents objected that this was contrary to feminist and child-centered pedagogy, because it restricted the imaginations of the children and encouraged them to think in traditional roles. Carole sided with these parents and asked Michelle to stop using the coloring books. The incident seemed to place the rhetoric of modern pedagogy in conflict with respect for African Americans, including one of our own teachers. The center called a parents' meeting with neither teacher present, and most of the attendees were white.

I was there as a parent and also as a researcher, and so was Linda. I found it difficult to listen to the discussion. It was ostensibly about pedagogy, but underneath the fine words, it was also about race and authority. The dominant pedagogical view was that Carole's approach was what "we" wanted. That's why we had hired her as lead teacher. Parents described Michelle as a good teacher, but "old fashioned." Several people spoke up for diversity in teaching approaches, including myself, but we were in the distinct minority. The opinion of the majority was that Michelle should be encouraged to teach the "other way," without the coloring books. I had a feeling that this would come to a bad end.

The next day, our board president told Michelle and Carole about the meeting and its conclusions. Two weeks later Michelle announced that she was leaving and would be taking another teaching job. No amount of cajoling could get her to change her mind. A month later the center hired a new black teacher who was younger and much more amenable to Carole's supervision.

This first failure in our multi-racial experiment was a big one. It showed that even though we could change books or toys or meals, deeper issues remained in our organization. We had not really addressed white privilege. Were we really creating new ways of living, or just producing a liberal surface on top of a discriminatory reality?

In this case, despite their children's equal numbers in the center, African American parents were less able to participate in decisions. In addition, the white and highly educated parents more eagerly embraced new views on child pedagogy. In part, these ideas coordinated well with the current anti-authoritarian views of well-educated women involved with feminism: "Let our children learn what they want...let them choose." This view tended to support the privileging of children who were used to reaching out and getting what they wanted, and it more often characterized the early socialization of white, rather than black, children. Furthering the possibility that parents would support the white teacher over the black one was the white-held notion that whites usually know more than blacks, part of the deep racism of America. Sometimes this idea is embedded in an essentialist biological view. At other times, it's fostered by a belief that culture and social structure create that difference. Could Michelle really know more than Carole if she didn't have Carole's masters degree in new approaches to pedagogy? Could her other teaching be more important than the question of coloring inside the lines sometimes? The majority of white parents could not really believe that these two things could be true.

The center survived, and it is still going strong in 2017. To my knowledge, no parents withdrew their children, although most of the mothers of the black and Hispanic children were upset. Both Linda and I kept our children there. Where else could we go? The white parents mostly wished that Michelle had stayed; some sympathized with her, while others felt justified in their views, interpreting her departure as a sign of her rigidity. Patty and I wrote up our research, which showed that the children had changed their play patterns over time. We never published it, though. Perhaps the contradictions were too great.

CHAPTER 21

HOW TO UNRAVEL A MARRIAGE

f a marriage is like a comfortable sweater, its unraveling begins with a loose thread. You pick at it, the string of wool drops further; you trim it, you make a repair, then you see a hole. Maybe you get out the needle and thread or a darning hook and close it up, because after all, a sweater is comfortable and expensive to replace. And it's still warm, even with a little loose stitching. Then one day, it feels just too shabby, and you start wearing it only as a backup or while gardening. One day you realize that a part of your sweater that you never seemed to notice, perhaps in the armpit, has a big gap. Now the back of the neck is unraveling. It's no longer possible to wash it without more threads coming loose. It is over. You have to throw it out, or maybe give it away, but even that isn't easy. Later you may wonder, was it ever beautiful?

That's how it was with my marriage. When Donald and I started going out in the fall of 1963, I hadn't recovered from my father's death that June. Fred Wallace, my previous boyfriend, had just dumped me definitively, because I was white and he knew he could never bring himself to marry across the race line. My mother was in her own mourning process; my two brothers were miles away. None of my close family was available to support me, and my friends in Cambridge seemed to be too engrossed in their own lives.

Donald, on the other hand, was attentive. He listened. I felt wanted. There were glitches from the start. He wasn't divorced yet, but he and his wife had separated. He was older by eleven years, 31 when I first met him, while I was a 20-year-old undergraduate. In those extra years, he had served in the Air Force, been briefly addicted to heroin, consumed lots of marijuana, and had many girlfriends. He was more sexually and culturally sophisticated than I was. While all these things had appeal, they also gave me some qualms. It wasn't always comfortable to be in a club where I was "the white girlfriend/lover." I was frequently treated dismissively, as the white outsider that I was.

When I went to work with SNCC full time in 1964, it had been partly to get away from him for a while. I had felt pulled in several directions at once: I thought I was a civil rights activist and a graduate student, but Donald's black friends seemed to see me primarily as the white girlfriend of a black guy. Perhaps there were ways that he and I weren't really a match. The problem, I think with 45 years of hindsight, may have been that I didn't even imagine the areas where the non-match would turn out to be most serious: child care, honesty about other relationships, and commitment to equality within the home.

After Gwendolyn's birth in 1968, our somewhat equal work at home had become a long downward slide for me. Despite multiple discussions, I never seemed to make any progress. I couldn't be as hardline as some friends suggested: "Just tell him you're going out and leave him with Gwendolyn, even if he objects!" My own desire for a neat home, with clean clothes for Gwen, made me incapable of waiting for him to get around to the dishes or the laundry.

We had moved to Hemenway Street in Boston in late spring of 1970. Our apartment was close to my job and to the Children's Center, and also near the South End, where Donald had worked before. In September, he was still looking for work, telling me that it was harder to find a job in the black social services nonprofit world because of our marriage and the Black Power critique of black men marrying white women. It could have been true, but there was a part of me that didn't believe it explained everything. Could he go back to picture framing, I wondered, and was he really looking?

We were living on my salary from Emmanuel and I was paying for the childcare. One day, Donald told me he was going to California. Was there work there? I don't remember the explanation. He left in late fall. One part of me was glad to see him go. I didn't feel appreciated and I was supporting him, while he was doing nothing to meet our domestic work agenda beyond adding some esthetic touches to our apartment.

A month passed, and then another. I began to hang out with Mike, the owner of an antiques store a block away. I would put Gwen in the stroller and walk over to chat and look at his collection of Native American beadwork and painted leather. In the crowded store we would sip tea, while he told me the stories of various objects and of his own family.

In early January, with Donald still away, a crisis hit. Gwendolyn came down with a high fever that just wouldn't break. A snowstorm lashed the city and dumped heavy snow everywhere. After four days of the fever and two visits to the doctor, I had to pick up some medicine at the pharmacy. I couldn't leave Gwendolyn to go get it, and I couldn't take her out, so I called Mike. Yes, he'd get it. That same afternoon, Donald called from California. I told him Gwendolyn was ill. He said he'd return, and I said, come on home. I was used to his being away, though. I didn't really care if he was home, since he was so useless in the unglamorous aspects of parenting.

At about 10 p.m., Mike came back with the prescription. I gave Gwen a dose, he sat and visited, we talked, and I felt so much in need, and so thankful that here was a person who *did* care about me and her, who would do all the things that Donald wouldn't. In an instant it was as if I fell in love with him, at least for that moment. We ended up in bed together. Kind of transgressive, of course, not only because I was married, but also because my daughter was ill in the room down the hall. And to top it off, I had a feeling that Donald might come back soon. Before getting into bed, I locked the door to the apartment from the inside, so having a key wouldn't be sufficient to enter.

Sure enough, at about 7:30 the next morning, while Mike and I were still in bed, I heard a key in the lock of our third-floor apartment. It was Donald. And there was no exit to the ground from our back door, which led only to a porch.

The ensuing confrontation was incredibly painful (no violence though), with Mike getting his clothes on and going out our door to the hallway while Donald stood in the living room. This was followed by more awkward and difficult discussion between Donald and myself. I apologized and said that I had no idea he was coming back so soon. He immediately began apologizing himself, saying it was all his fault. This confused me. For the first time, I wondered if there was a woman in California. He said something about going away and leaving me alone for so long. He then asked me to take a bath, and to my surprise and disgust, wanted to have sex.

✦

As Donald settled back into life in Boston, we discussed our future. He asked me to promise not to sleep with Mike again, and I agreed. And about a month later, a much better place to live appeared in a different part of town. That reduced the temptation considerably and also brought us closer to two people I admired and liked a lot.

John and Amanda Perdew had just bought a two-family house on Crawford St. in Roxbury. Large houses built in the early 1900s were shaded by mature trees in this black, middle-class area. Families passed the houses down from one generation to the next. This was the Boston equivalent of Harlem's Sugar Hill. John and Amanda had been lucky to buy a house in the center of the nicest block on Crawford.

The Perdews had met in Albany, Georgia in the early sixties. She was a black high school student leader of the Albany Movement, and he was a white Harvard student from Colorado. Like so many interracial couples spawned in the intense months of demonstrations and organizing, they first admired each other and then fell in love. They married (probably in Colorado, as it would have been illegal in Georgia) and moved to the Boston area in 1966. Their first child, Natasha, was born in 1967, and their second, Tambwe, in 1969. They invited us to join them on Crawford St., where we would rent the upstairs apartment.

This was an almost ideal arrangement. A grand open staircase connected our apartments, and because we knew each other, we usually kept our doors open during the day. Amanda was often home, and our children played together frequently. In a world of divisions – even in Boston – it was consoling and supporting to share space with another interracial couple, especially a couple with whom we shared politics and both past and future commitments to activism.

From Amanda, I learned how to teach my daughter to share with other children. Watching both her and John, I was also reminded that a man can share everything in childrearing and housework, and that it can seem normal. It was as if I had forgotten that during the previous two years of domestic struggle with Donald.

I wish we could have shared the house forever, but it was

not to be. Donald and I continued to argue over his responsibilities at home. (I closed the doors to the staircase for this.) Finally I told him I couldn't take it any more.

"Either you change or we have to separate," I said. No answer.

I can't remember if we discussed divorce, per se. We had challenged so much to get and stay together that it was really hard to think about a public admission that our proud act had failed. Maybe a separation would produce some change. I just couldn't stand what I was going through. I thought that even if divorce were the final outcome, I had to stop living with him right now. I was feeling depressed and stuck.

Who would move? From the start, we assumed that I would be the primary parent. I thought I should stay in the apartment where we were living. Donald said he should stay because, after all, this was the black community and he was black. He belonged here more than I did. But I pointed out there was another white person on this street – John – and he lived in this building. And Gwen was just as black or "mixed" as Tambwe and Tasha. She and I would both be here. Did we really have to move?

Rather than argue and have Donald continue to camp at our apartment as a self-righteous live-in, I decided to discuss it with Amanda and John. After all, it was their house. To my relief, and boosting my self-esteem, they were adamant. Of course Nancy should stay, they said. She's taking care of Gwen, and it's much easier for Donald to move. It was settled, and he moved in early spring, 1971. I was halfway through my first year of teaching at Emmanuel, and still months short of finishing the first draft of my dissertation.

I felt happy at Crawford St., but it didn't last. Amanda wanted to move back to the South, and when John got a job in Atlanta, they decided to leave. A young African American woman with a son Gwen's age bought the house, and I had to find a new place to live. I was about to leave the first of our six different homes in a one-year period.

My friend Louise, a single mother, lived in what had once been her parents' home on a shady street in Cambridgeport. Her son, Lucas, another interracial child, was a year older than Gwen. In exchange for some babysitting and some rent, she offered us a bedroom off her living room.

In what would become a pattern, my friend Marty Gopen, a sweet Jewish guy who I'd known from the early Boston Action Group days, drove over to Crawford St. in his 1964 Ford Country Squire station wagon. We loaded it with books, clothes, pots and pans, and a little furniture. This, together with what I could fit into my two-door Toyota Corolla, came with me to Cambridgeport. Everything else went to Donald, or was given to charity. Since there wasn't too much space in our new personal room, I convinced Louise to let me store some things in the basement.

Gwen and I settled in and lived there for about three months. She continued at the Children's Center, her days stable, even if her evenings and nights had changed. During this period, Donald and I tried to reconcile. We talked with a white couple who were both therapists, and somehow, they convinced us to try living together again. Louise's tenant upstairs was moving early in June, and it was agreed that Donald and I would move up to her furnished attic apartment: it had a living room, a kitchen, and a tiny bathroom. There was also a small bedroom for Gwen, and a little study where I could work on my dissertation. Donald and I would sleep in the living room in an alcove.

So in mid-June, I moved up and Donald moved in. On the first day, my belief that we should try to "get back together" was jolted with a feeling of shock and distress. I didn't want to have sex. The idea repelled me. Even sleeping in the same bed was hard. I lay stiffly, trying not to touch. Why hadn't I thought about this during those months apart? Why hadn't we tried to have sex? I don't think we had even kissed or held hands. We had become a shell family, looking like a threesome, but with an open space between the two adults where love and desire should have, or could have, been. I was angry. I knew it wasn't Donald's fault especially. We were living out a shadow play, and I couldn't get comfortable enough to even talk with him about it.

That first night, I knew that our marriage was really over. On the other hand, I couldn't stand the thought of moving immediately.

Emmanuel was on vacation until September; I had two months off from teaching and had full-time childcare, paid for from my savings from my nine-month salary. I would stick it out here. I dropped Gwendolyn off every morning and picked her up in the afternoon. In the narrow study, with a converted door as a desk and two six-foot bookshelves above it, I wrote five days a week, from 9 a.m. to 3 p.m. for six weeks, creating a full first draft of my thesis. I had told myself I had to write a chapter a week, and each one had to be about twenty pages. By late August, I had 140 pages, which I edited and re-edited during the coming academic year. Thank the goddesses for the Children's Center and the kindness of friends!

Each evening Donald and I visited, hung out with our daughter, and had dinner. After all, we were still some kind of a family. Although we were polite to each other, inside I was yearning for an escape. At the same time, I was angry at myself for moving in together, even though some part of me had already known that I wasn't ready (and might never be ready). I was harming him, as well as myself, by encouraging him to think that it might work. I must have discussed this somewhere, somehow, with someone, but I don't remember it. It was a shameful secret.

Finally the escape route appeared. Richard Yarde, that old

friend of Donald's and Gwen's godfather, had recently gotten a job at Wellesley teaching art. The college had given him and his family a large house just off campus to live in. Richard and Susan were another interracial couple, he from Barbados and she from a New England Irish background. Their children, Marcus and Owen, bracketed Gwendolyn in age, just like Tasha and Tambwe had. They had extra space in their college home. After I had some conversations with Susan about my living situation, she and Richard invited Gwendolyn and me to live there, rent free. I gladly took up the offer. I liked them both, and their children were delicious: funny, creative, and busy. I told Donald that I really didn't think we could live together. I was sorry, but it was over.

So that fall, perhaps in early September, I made my third move of the year, this time to a beautiful location about fifteen miles from work. For the second time, Marty Gopen helped me move, using his station wagon to complement my Toyota. While I didn't like moving, I was both thankful and proud that we could do everything with two carloads. Years later, Marty told me he had been glad to help me because he knew that Donald had been seeing other women throughout our marriage. Marty expressed surprise that I hadn't known. I wished that he, or others, had told me. It would have made my guilt a lot less.

At Susan and Richard's, Gwen and I had a small suite consisting of a hall, two rooms, and a bath. We shared the Yarde kitchen in the larger part of the century-old house. It sounded good, but turned out to be an untenable mix.

Both Richard and Susan had workspaces at home. Richard's was an art studio, where he prepared large, glowing watercolors referencing black history. His 3' x 6' painting of Daddy Grace was decorated with the flowers of church, while an equally large portrait of Marcus Garvey showed the black activist with the red, green, and black banners of the UNIA. Susan had a study where she wrote her poetry.

Each parent would go into their own private space (often at the same time), lock their doors, and disappear into work. While a room of one's own sounds good, neither was willing to interrupt creative time for either of their young children unless there was an emergency and much crying and door pounding. As a result, Marcus and Owen, ages four and two, essentially tore up their toys and the rest of the first floor of the house. (My apartment upstairs was off limits.) A view from the doorway into their children's bedroom revealed two mattresses on the floor, with blankets and old sheets loosely strewn around. The floor itself was covered with many pieces of plastic, metal, wood, paper, crayons, fabric, and food. Closer examination revealed that these little items were the leftover bits of toys, clothes, and meals.

In my apartment, by contrast, when Gwen was home, I was also there keeping an eye on her and encouraging her to play with her toys in such a way that they would last. We sat at a table for meals, I changed her clothes daily, and she helped clean up her play space and room each day. This is how I had been raised, and I repeated it with my daughter. It also reflected the general philosophy of the Children's Center, where she continued to spend her days.

Richard and Susan loved their children deeply, but we had very different ideas of parenting. In order to create a compromise or peace between my child and theirs, I encouraged all three children to play together (a very easy task, including both interactive and parallel play in our space and theirs) when I was there, and also tried to give the parents some extra time by helping with snacks and other child needs whenever I was home.

In another difference between us, their approach to money was to take Richard's paycheck at the end of the month and spend luxuriously on all the things they might have missed.

Mine was to carefully budget so I never ran out. On the first of the month, Susan would make a beautiful meal: steak, truffles, expensive wine, and an elegant dessert. Similarly, they each bought the other expensive birthday and Christmas presents, even if they had to wear worn-out clothes and eat Rice-a-Roni for days on end.

Despite our affection for each other, Richard and Susan's hands-off approach to daytime child supervision, combined with their exuberant approach to holidays (the first of the month, birthdays, Christmas) was a contrast to my much more controlled, almost ascetic approach. The first inevitable crisis erupted just before Christmas. I can laugh about it now, but then, I was shaken and disturbed.

It was about a week before Christmas. I wanted to bring some of the atmosphere which was usual in the Shaw extended family, and which had existed in Donald's and my previous apartments, into the house. Susan and Richard liked to wait until Christmas Eve for everything: the tree, decorations, and presents. In a compromise, I suggested, and they accepted, that I would put up a small tree in our space a little early. So Gwen and I got a little fir and decorated it with our bulbs and some popcorn strings. Marcus and Owen helped.

The next day, I drove to Emmanuel to turn in my fall semester grade sheets. Late in the afternoon, I picked up Gwendolyn at the Children's Center and drove back to Wellesley and our home. Everything seemed normal until I opened the door to our living room. Something was missing. It was the Christmas tree! I was sure I had left it right there in the morning. What had happened? It didn't seem to be in another room.

Inquiries to both parents and the children in the rest of the house produced nothing.

"No."

"Nope."

"I don't know."

I started opening closet doors, and there, in a back hallway, was the tree! It had been dragged from my living room and "put away" by Marcus and Owen because "the tree doesn't go up until Christmas."

I could see that Gwen and I were disturbing the normal routines of the household. I thought, okay, I'll just try to fit in a little better.

This hope came to an end about six weeks later. Susan liked to let her canary out of his cage so he could fly around the kitchen. For these periods, she kept her 12-year-old cat out of the room as much as possible. I did the same with Waldo, our tabby. Opening the cage door was usually followed by closing the kitchen door to keep the canary safe. One day, the little bird was missing.

The ultimate conclusion: Waldo did it. The older cat wasn't a leaper, and Waldo had somehow gained access to the room. We even saw a few feathers. Susan was devastated, and although she wanted to get a new bird (which I offered to pay for), she really couldn't see getting another bird if Waldo stayed with us.

Post-ultimate conclusion: I knew I couldn't continue to live there.

Fortunately, Crawford St. came through again to save us. Lynette, the temporary tenant downstairs had moved. Would I like to rent the first floor for a year or more? Yes!

With Marty's assistance once again, I loaded up and moved back to Roxbury, where Gwen and I spent our last year in Boston. During that year, Donald and I completed our divorce, even though he refused to participate beyond reading the materials sent by my lawyer.

CHAPTER 22

MOVING ON

n May 1972, I defended my thesis at Brandeis. Nine years after
I had entered graduate school, I could legitimately call myself
Dr. Nancy Stoller Shaw. It had taken far longer than the ideal
five years of graduate study. Moving ahead on my degree every year had been such a struggle. I felt as if half my adult life
had passed me by. The standard I judged myself by, however,
had been created with a man in mind. That man had economic
support (a wealthy family or fellowships) and no birthing or
childrearing responsibilities. If married, he had a wife to make
his meals, clean his clothes, and take care of any children who
appeared.

I had been raised to believe that I could live my life with
all the privileges of a boy. I thought my family modeled equality between the sexes. (I conveniently overlooked my mother's
time in the kitchen while I was admiring my father's aerospace
work, and his seat in the easy chair reading files and engineering journals.) I never realized that I would run into so many ob-
stacles as soon as I gave birth. Because of my label as a "mother"
I was expected to take on almost all the responsibilities for my

child. No aspect of graduate school was made "easier" for me. I did benefit directly from feminism, Boston NOW, and the Children's Center. These groups, and one of my childhood masculine characteristics, helped me survive and get my degree: I relied on tenacity and a refusal to believe that I couldn't meet any physical, social, and intellectual challenge at which a male could succeed. I had been stubborn and successful when my Stonewall self hoisted her body to the top magnolia branch, ran for the first down in the Braxton's backyard, or slogged for five hours in the rain in the Blue Ridge Mountains. I think I channeled that stubbornness as a civil rights activist and again in graduate school, when I moved and moved and got divorced, and drove my daughter to day care week after week and still continued to teach and research and write and revise my dissertation. Ultimately, I won.

As I think back, maybe nine years wasn't so long, given what I had to go through. My struggle and success were the same ones reflected in the punch line of the Fred Astaire/Ginger Rogers joke: "She did all the steps just like he did, only backwards and in high heels." Doing double the work to get where the guys got in the university world turned out to be good practice for the emotional, political, and social challenges I would face when I went up for tenure nine years later.

A few weeks after my dissertation defense, one of my professors asked me to see him during his office hours. Would I let him publish my thesis in the new series he was editing for Pergamon Press? *Let* him? Of course! I was ecstatic. It took almost two years before the book made it to the bookstores, but I probably had one of the easier paths to publication that a doctoral student could traverse in 1972: from holding a just-bound dissertation to seeing it advertised in the catalog of a prominent scientific publisher and displayed as a real book in stores.

I could feel my life turning around. I had been living

through a really messy period, which I now think might have started with my father's death. That loss had led me into my relationship with Donald, which was never as idyllic as I had hoped it would be. Now, ten years after the start of our relationship, our divorce was complete and the six-month waiting period marking when one could remarry almost over. Getting married, however, was something I could not imagine ever repeating.

I was feeling increasingly separate and secure from intrusions by Donald into my personal life. He continued to call me, and would occasionally show up outside my apartment, but his contacts became less frequent, devolving into his twice-a-month weekend visits with Gwendolyn. I did still see him at family functions, like Thanksgiving and Christmas, with other Shaws.

The way the Shaw world worked, once you were a member with a child, you stayed a member. Or more accurately, your child was a member, and since women did all important parenting, the child's mother was also a part of the family network. Being a white parent was no impediment to joining this extended black family. In those days, Shaw family social life was centered around Donald's sister, Eunice Joanna. A secondary circle met at Sarah Ann Shaw's house. She had been Donald's first wife, the mother of Gwendolyn's step-sister Klare (by a different father). Gwendolyn and I would join the whole family at Sarah Ann's for Thanksgiving dinner. We observed Christmas at Joanna's. Everyone thought it normal that all the exes and their children were present. It didn't seem to matter that Gerald's wife, Sally, or I were white; what counted was how we acted and our connections through our children.

Even though I was no longer married to a Shaw, I knew I wanted and needed to stay connected to the family because Gwendolyn needed her African American family perhaps more than she needed my white family. Further, I lived close to the Shaws and the Stollers were all in other cities. My own biological family spread out between Maryland and Colorado, with one brother in Vietnam for a while. For some holidays, Gwendolyn and I would go to my mother's house in Maryland, where she lived with her second husband. I felt – and still feel – like a permanent part of the Shaw family.

After Gwendolyn and I relocated to California, with Donald on the East Coast and elsewhere, I did what I could to get Gwen to the Shaw households in Boston, and to visit myself. Thirty years later, when Joanna developed early Alzheimer's, the family links began to loosen. Back in 1972 and '73, though, the network remained strong, and Boston was its home.

In 1972, we had a wide family extending into both the black and white world. Even though Donald couldn't take away my apartment because he was black and the apartment was in a black neighborhood, he didn't want to exile me from the family I had married into. Even if he couldn't care directly for Gwendolyn, he did want to see her, and we both wanted her to grow up with as much black culture as possible. For me, this meant visiting the Shaw family often, and that meant I had to see Donald repeatedly at both small and big family functions, even though I kept wishing I would never see him and that people wouldn't ask about him when they saw me.

Everything he did seemed tacky and unappealing. I began to dislike his clothes, his interest in sports, and his style of talking. I was angry with him for not compromising so we could stay together. At the same time, I was angry with myself that I had been married to him for so long. Why had it taken me so long to get loose? Then I felt shame about being angry. I knew he wasn't all bad. At the same time, I loved Gwendolyn and was glad Donald and I had gotten together to create her. And I felt we did it the right way: getting married, giving her his name...I went back and forth in my thinking.

However, I lacked the effective therapy, or emotional so-phistication, to figure out all these conflicting thoughts. I set-tled on wishing he would just go away. I tried out some other relationships, first with my lawyer, and then with a local radical who worked with me on the *Science for the People* 'zine. Donald wouldn't disappear. Boston seemed too small. Increasingly, I was happiest when I was out of town, so I began to find ways to escape from Boston. These trips turned into both escapes and a discovery of a new aspect of myself.

When I had been hired at Emmanuel in 1970, there had been a student interview committee. One of the members was a senior, Nina Fortin. Although she graduated before I began to teach, I got to know her through a mutual friendship network, which included several students who were still at the college. One of them babysat for me. By spring of 1971, Nina was also babysitting. I began to visit more with her. It was all strictly pla-tonic. She had a boyfriend, who I rarely saw, and I was dating various men.

As Nina and I spent more time together, though, we joked that it was too bad that we each had to save alternate weekends to be with our boyfriends, when we would have preferred to be with each other.

In the summer of 1972, she and I took a vacation trip with Gwendolyn to Prince Edward Island in eastern Canada to camp for five days.

We brought a huge tent with two rooms, something that a friend of Nina's had gotten from an Army surplus store. I would put Gwendolyn to sleep in the early evening in the back room. Nina and I would then stay up talking or reading in the front. I didn't know it yet, but I was falling in love.

One night, we were camped on a beach. There was a huge windstorm, and the tent kept flailing around and falling inward. We piled our luggage around the inside edges. Gwendolyn just slept on while we fretted and shifted bags and boxes. Despite worrying that our tent might blow over sideways, I was completely happy to be there. The next day, we laughed repeatedly as we imitated the snapping, flapping, cracking sounds of the tent and retold our panicked moments.

Another day, we found a long-roped swing on a high tree on the hill overlooking our campsite. We took turns swinging ourselves and pushing Gwen. I remember being high in the air, as high as I could go. I was looking down on the grassy hill with its scattered daisies toward my two companions. Just beyond was a river. I felt both exhilarated and calm. Everything was beautiful. My funny, curious daughter was near me, playing with someone I trusted completely, who was also entertaining her so she laughed and giggled.

✦

Nina was living in her hometown, Pawtucket, Rhode Island, about an hour away from Boston. We organized our lives around weekends: when I had Gwen for the weekend, she would usually do something with her boyfriend. When Gwen was with Donald, I might visit Nina in Pawtucket, sharing her bedroom (twin beds) and smoking dope while her mother smiled in the living room and seemed to have no idea what her daughter was up to. Other child-free weekends might find us camping nearby.

On a weekend trip in rural Massachusetts, we were in a renovated barn loft. There was only one bed, and we were close together under a thick quilt. The moon shone in through a window just above our heads. Very romantic. I wanted to snuggle up as close as I could, but I knew that would be crossing a boundary that had never been even discussed in our friendship. I couldn't just "do it." I didn't want to risk rejection. And even though I was capable of lots of denial and ignorance, I knew that my attraction was similar to my attraction to a guy. It was erotic. Even though I didn't see anything wrong with it, I had no idea if she felt the same way. Still, the pull was inescapable. I had to do something. We had just said good night, and she was turned away, about to sleep.

"Nina," I said, "I want you to know, I'm physically attracted to you."

No response. Nothing.

"Nina?"

"Hmm. That's okay."

Nothing else.

I was afraid to say anything more. I just lay there. Was she rejecting me gently? Was she saying, "I like you as a friend, but something more doesn't interest me"? Or maybe the idea of attraction interested her, but she didn't want anything to happen. Or did she think I was weird? Or was it that she didn't know how to talk about it? If she felt like I did, she certainly didn't say so. She was never very good about expressing her feelings. And she had been brought up in a Catholic household, and went to Catholic school all the way through college...

Later, I thought she was just too repressed for either a discussion or any touching. That night, I decided, "Well, that was a bust." The next day, we said nothing. We continued our friendship.

A few months later, I tried again.

"Nina, I'm still attracted to you."

"That's okay. We can be friends."

Well, that was a definite rejection. I decided to give up. My love was unrequited, but I still had a boyfriend for sex, and I'd have Nina for everything else. This set the pattern for our closeness for the next few years, spending time together while having male lovers.

Getting to know Nina while working at Emmanuel and

living in Boston had been a great present for me. She'll always be the first adult I consider that I really fell deeply in love with. And of course she was also the first woman I was erotically attracted to.

My bonds to Boston were lessening. My mother and her second husband had decided to move from Maryland to San Diego, a place with nice weather for an older couple. Her husband's former employer, the CIA, would pay all their retirement moving expenses. With both of my brothers now living in Colorado (just across the street from each other, a pattern of closeness they have maintained their entire lives), an important part of my family was shifting westward.

Graduate school was over, and my cohort was beginning to move to new locations. My marriage was also over and I didn't like being near my ex. I wanted a better job at a research university. I needed to get out of town.

When I closed my eyes and imagined a future, I was back on Prince Edward Island with Gwendolyn and Nina, floating on that long-roped swing, looking down that hill to the river.

It wasn't just the view of the hillside and the river that soothed me. The scene was imbued with happiness and peace. When I was there, I felt I was exactly where I wanted to be, and both the adult and the child who were with me were exactly the people I wanted most to be with.

Gwendolyn and I got in our 1965 Dodge Charger, and headed west across America. We headed toward a job offer at UC Santa Cruz and that feeling of being high in the air, as high as I could go. Maybe we would never have perfect stability. But through love and through direct action, we would find our balance—and keep "making up" new paths, to freedom.

ABOUT THE AUTHOR

NANCY STOLLER was born in 1942 in Newport News, Virginia, near North Carolina. In 1960, she left Virginia to attend Wellesley College where she earned an A.B. in Philosophy in 1963, and awarded a Phi Beta Kappa. For five years in the 1960s, she was a volunteer and a field secretary for the Student Nonviolent Coordinating Committee. Stoller went on to earn her M.A. (1965) and Ph.D. (1972) in Sociology from Brandeis University in Waltham, Massachusetts. From 1978-1980 she was a Post-doctoral fellow at Yale University. Stoller started her job at University of California (UC) Santa Cruz in 1973 and received tenure in 1987 after having successfully filed a gender discrimination suit against the University. Stoller worked and published under her married name, Nancy Shaw, for many years before returning to her family name, Stoller, in the 1990s. Along with her work on AIDS, Stoller's research has focused on AIDS healthcare and politics, women in prison, and health care. Among many publications, Stoller is a co-editor of *Women Resisting AIDS: Feminist Strategies of Empowerment*, the editor of Women and AIDS Clinical Resource Guide, and the author of *Lessons From the Damned: Queers, Whores, and Junkies Respond to AIDS*. This is her first memoir.

58086517R00126

Made in the USA
Columbia, SC
18 May 2019